Praise for *Leadership in Groups*

"[A] remarkable achievement…[Newton] adroitly applies…[his] unique framework and his extensive experience to solve the difficult people problems confronting…almost all organizations…. Moreover, he accomplishes this with prose that is readable, enjoyable and jargon-free."

—Maurice G. Marcus, M.D.

Psychoanalyst and Consultant, Boswell Group

"Nearly every chapter of this fine book addresses an issue that I face as a manager on a weekly basis…. Dr. Newton understands the predicament of the law firm manager and provides extremely valuable insight and much appreciated humor."

—Daniel E. Cohn, J.D., Chairman,

Commercial Department, Farella, Braun & Martel, LLP

"A must read….Those who read this book will be better able to successfully address the challenges facing their firms."

—William S. Klein, J.D., Managing Shareholder

Hopkins & Carley, PC

Leadership in Groups

A Casebook

Dr. Peter M. Newton

ISBN: 978-1517062057

Printed in the United States of America
First Edition, 2015
Second Edition, 2022

Other Books by Dr. Peter M. Newton

Non-Fiction

Freud: From Youthful Dream to Mid-Life Crisis. New York: Guilford Press, 1995.

Unorthodox Freud: The View From the Couch (with Lohser). New York: Guilford Press, 1996.

Waypoints to a New Life: Learning to Sail at Fifty, 2019.

Fiction

Colchester, A Novel, 2022.

Dedication

For my father, Warren Sanford Newton, who was a competent and humane manager and let me watch him work. And for my mentor, Daniel J. Levinson, who taught me how to use a social psychological imagination in the understanding of organizational life.

And, for Julie Chu Meng, whose sense of humor conquers all.

Acknowledgements

I want to thank Amelia Newton for her editorial assistance throughout the writing of this book, including but not limited to the creation of the index. I would also like to thank Jeffrey Kaye, Maurice Marcus, Charles Sink and Gail Hashimoto for their review of drafts of my Management Thoughtletter out of which some parts of this book grew.

I would also like to thank the organizational leaders who allowed me to learn about them and their work and the kindness of the several who became my friends.

"Organization is the means through which an enterprise secures the performance of its tasks."

E. J. Miller & A. K. Rice, *Systems of Organization*

Table of Contents

Foreword

Of my 20 partner retreats, I remember one most distinctly. Peter Newton spoke for two hours to our 60 partners on mentoring, on retaining associates, and on the different phases of a lawyer's career. The whole two hours, no one checked their email or talked with the person next to them. Rapt attention the whole time.

Dr. Newton covers the same territory, and much more of the legal landscape, in *Leadership in Groups*. Unlike any other book on organization or management, this one is a pleasure to read. The author enjoys writing, so that you may avoid clunky terminology and wooden exposition of law firm dynamics and individual attorney behavior. Dr. Newton says more in these relatively few pages than any other author in the field does. He evidently expects us to understand, the first time he says it. And, you will.

As English journalists, historians and writers have a gift for explaining Americans to ourselves, so does Dr. Newton. Moreover, he combines insight with compassion for the profession. He seeks to cure what so often ails our profession and our personal experience of it. You simply cannot help seeing the legal firm and practice of law differently after this remarkable book. An essay for the thinking lawyer, the harried group manager and the attorney wondering how their profession could be more satisfying. I enthusiastically recommend it.

Charles M. Sink, J.D.

Preface

This book arises from 40 some years of experience consulting with diverse groups and organizations. These enterprises have included hospitals, clinics, government and community mental health agencies, labor unions, construction, technology, investment, manufacturing, telecommunications, marketing, and publishing companies, start-ups of various kinds, and law firms ranging in size from small to large. The clients have ranged in authority from board chairmen, through CEOs and managing partners, to human resources managers and executive secretaries.

It also issues from my experience of having been a graduate school dean, a faculty chairman, and a clinic director and from having directed numerous large residential conferences on group relations.

Beginning in 1968, I taught graduate seminars in organizational structure and group dynamics at Columbia, Yale, the University of Washington, UC Berkeley, and the Wright Institute. These academic institutions provided support for my research in adult development and organizational life, which forms part of the conceptual and empirical foundation for this book.

During the past ten years or so, most of my consulting work has been with law firms in the US and Canada. These firms have varied in size from quite small to very large. My work with law firms began as a consultant with Hildebrandt International, the legal consulting firm. Later I formed my own company.

Like many psychologists, my early interest and training emphasized psychopathology and psychotherapy, although I always had an interest in social psychology. It was my great good fortune that the graduate program I entered at Columbia University in 1964 taught both clinical psychology and group dynamics.

This was a time of social movement and unrest, and groups were seen as a force for progressive change, if not its embodiment. The spirit was idealistic and communitarian, far different from the isolated narcissism into which we later lapsed and in which we continue to exist, as of this writing. Plugged into our laptops and iPhone, with no collective goals beyond avoiding terrorism, we seem to have become an aggregate of sovereign monads.

In 1968 students occupied several buildings at Columbia to protest the Vietnam War. This created a crisis of authority within my school, as it did in some others. My department at Columbia hired Daniel Levinson to consult with us about the structure and functioning of leadership and authority in our group.

In the mid-1960s, Daniel Levinson and other influential American psychologists and psychiatrists had gone to England to learn about the new thinking and training in group relations going on at the Tavistock Centre in London.

Based upon their own experience managing and consulting to industries in Great Britain and abroad, the English were doing something new and intellectually exciting. Under the leadership of A. K. Rice, E. J. Miller, Wilfred Bion, Elliott Jaques and others, social scientists and psychoanalysts were uniting a social system approach to enterprises with a psychodynamic conception of individuals and groups.

This combined approach constituted a conceptual breakthrough in social science, as would Levinson's later work on adult development in psychology.

Like other marriages, this one was not perfect. Most of its offspring chose one parent over the other, usually preferring the psychodynamic side. It did, however, provide the means for solving a longstanding conceptual problem that had kept separate the lines of thought needed to understand groups.

Narrow training, guild prejudices and territoriality had kept the disciplines of sociology, psychology, and psychoanalysis at arm's length. The result was a psychologically superficial sociology of groups and a naively individualistic psychology that focused exclusively upon the individual, or at best the pair, in an unexplained group setting.

The sociological view saw individuals simply as representatives of categories—e.g., race, class, gender (litigator, tax lawyer)—and stereotyped them.

Application of the individual psychology approach lent itself to scapegoating of individuals. With this approach one failed to recognize when the group was covertly inducing the behavior which it called objectionable. In the law firm, an example would be the egoism of senior partners with large books of business, whose flouting of the firm culture is subtly encouraged by other partners as a challenge to the managing partner's authority.

Levinson did not accept the splitting of the sociological from the psychological and neither have I. Regarding the relationship between individual and group, he liked to quote the playwright Arthur Miller, "the fish is in the water and the water is in the fish."

I left Columbia to work with Levinson and others at Yale in this new English group psychology. Levinson is now best known for his work in adult development, but he was only just beginning it when I met him in 1969. His primary interest then was in the structure and functioning of organizations.

Happily, I learned both from him, and at so young an age and in so rich a mentor relationship, that each perspective—organizational structure and dynamics *and* adult development—was deeply internalized. The reader will find the two views integrated throughout this book, especially in the chapter on careers across the life span.

While many of the case examples are drawn from the modern North American law firm, they draw upon my experience in consulting with different kinds of enterprises, too. Readers who work in other organizations, especially other professional service organizations (e.g., medical, academic, financial, technology), should find little difficulty in applying the conceptual approach and many of the recommendations to their own settings. Notions such as *good values rationalizations, task displacement, generative supervision, authentic mentor relationships, a facilitating structure, leader-follower emotional feedback loops, competent followership, and a culture of learning and development* vs. *a culture of criticism and blame* are applicable generally and badly needed.

Perhaps a word or two is necessary to explain why a psychologist would want to help a law firm. A marginally solvent psychology colleague or two wanted such answers as I made my annual professor's salary in a single month of consulting. The simple answers are these: Law firms suffer from a problem I know how to solve and pay unstintingly for real solutions.

Law schools do not teach lawyers how to organize firms, any more than medical schools teach doctors how to organize hospitals. In the beginnings, lawyers set about busily doing difficult legal work. Their firms grow not by design but by the press of business. In time, attorneys find themselves enmeshed in working arrangements with other lawyers that have no other premise than that they follow the example of other mindlessly constructed firms. Bad structure puts people at odds and running into other people while working on difficult matters under great billable hour pressure is maddening. As they have no way of thinking about organizational structure, they blame each other.

Thus, their problems are problems of leadership and organizational structure and I had been studying these all of my professional life.

If their problem was generally suffered, each nonetheless had its own distinctive features and required tailor made, not off the rack solutions. Thus, each involved the conduct of a case study, where the case was not a problematic partner, but a dysfunctional structure. How is the work structured—practice groups, departments—and how is it led—practice group leaders, department heads, executive committee, managing partners? I interviewed partners about their roles in the firm, made extensive notes, studied them, then presented findings and recommendations. It was highly paid action research, that is research that led to concrete changes.

Highly paid? As I was as senior and as accomplished in my own profession as they were in theirs, I charged what a firm's senior partners charged. After fifteen years and many invoices, I had had only two questioned and, upon explanation, both were paid.

I should also add that I liked most of the attorneys I worked with. I found them sane, responsible, cooperative, and grateful for real help. It's true that many attorneys are required to be aggressive in their professional roles, but most are not especially aggressive when not in role. Many are conflict avoidant, and some are shy, even sensitive.

My high fees and the fact that I was contacted by people who knew themselves to be insufficiently competent at managing their firms may have shielded me from a lower level of grasping and unscrupulous attorneys with personalities indistinguishable from their professional roles.

The many case examples in this book are meant to bring its conceptual principles to life. Though most are taken from the law firm, the human problems they depict are common, even at core, universal; e.g., the movement of the individual up the generational ladder, the differentiation and integration of system structure, the problem of leadership and the exercise of authority. With the exception of the H-P Case, which is derived solely from published newspaper articles, the cases within are fictionalized. The events are real but the firms are disguised, as are some immaterial aspects of persons. All locations are changed.

Introduction

Why do people dislike attorneys, including attorneys, more than members of the other professions such as physicians and professors. First, they make too much money, on average twice that of physicians and three times that of professors. What can the justification possibly be for charging ten dollars a minute? In many cases, the explanation is simply that that is what other attorneys charge.

In addition to being obscenely overpaid, attorneys are in possession of arcane knowledge that can be employed in the destruction of lay persons, who can only defend themselves by hiring similarly overpaid lawyers. It has been said that the only society worse than one with too many attorneys is one with too few. Not surprisingly this observation was put forward by an attorney. Currently the US has some three times per capita the number of attorneys in England. If there weren't so many attorneys, it wouldn't be necessary to have so many attorneys.

As an organization, the law firm is an interesting place full of bright, busy people who make a lot of money doing challenging work. In this way it is similar to a hospital and, though salaries are far higher, to a university or to an investment or technology company. All are professional service organizations in which the "line workers" are highly trained professionals who have been socialized in their graduate educations to hold high standards of practice and to discharge their responsibilities autonomously. In the organizational setting, they may find it difficult to cooperate with others and to accept management.

Occasionally some portion of a law firm retreat is dedicated to deepening appreciation of personality differences among partners with an eye towards enhancing cooperation. Occasionally, consultants are brought in to administer personality tests. Typically, the tests employed have little demonstrated validity and are interpreted by people who have little or no professional training in personality assessment.

Although the portraits that these tests draw are far too simple, it can yet be regarded as a step forward if attorneys emerge from the exercise recognizing that their partners may see and react to things differently for good reasons. An increased understanding of psychology also helps attorneys better manage their relations with clients.

Realistic Assessment of Personality

In actuality, psychology in the law firm and other groups is more complicated than popular tests can reveal and is the result of multiple determinants. Motivation and behavior, as well as the meaning of work, are largely determined by an *interaction* of personality type, means of production, generational position, and organizational role. I will have more to say about this in Chapter One.

Let it suffice here to say that obsessive compulsive personality is the modal—not universal—personality configuration in the law firm, as in other professional service firms. While each of us has obsessive compulsive trends in his personality, these trends are reinforced in the lawyer's personality by the highly technical nature of most legal work, the rapid production that is required, and because the costs of the work and of error are so great.

The requirement in most forms of legal work to maintain reasonable relations with clients means that the incidence of debilitating psychopathology among private practice lawyers is low—perhaps ten percent. What we find typically are not debilitated persons but encumbered ones. In other organizations where the professional is protected or kept from the client, as for example in the research university, the incidence of serious psychopathology such as schizoid personality appears higher.

Serious mental illness is not a factor in most law firms—unless, of course, a truly deformed individual succeeds in becoming head of a major department or managing partner of the whole firm. Here the possibilities of general demoralization and even ruin rise worrisomely.

As noted, personality is not everything in accounting for meaning and behavior. It is necessary also to take the means of production, generational position and organizational role—associate, partner, department head, managing partner, senior lawyer—into consideration. If we add gender and ethnicity as factors, we will have accounted for most of what can be explained about the behavior of lawyers in law firms.

The Billable Hour

As noted, legal work sold by the hour is the means of production and an important determinant of psychology in the law firm. In American law firms as of this writing, the median salary for partners in good firms is about 400K and the billable hour rate about 500 dollars. These numbers vary from market to market and will be somewhat higher in New York City and lower in Denver. Among American Lawyer 100 firms, they double. The median income of associates is roughly 200K.

The managing partner gives lawyers billable hour targets each year. Eighteen hundred and fifty hours is a common goal. To make this target, a lawyer will have to bill more than seven hours per day (7+ hours times 22.5 working days a month times 11 months a year). N.B: He or she must not just work over seven hours a day, but *bill* that many hours. Two thirty minute dithers about what to do next, one off the clock conversation with a colleague, two trips to the bathroom, and lunch put the attorney behind the eight ball. A partner told me that when young he had taken a two week vacation and found upon return that he had lost most of his clients. He never took a vacation again.

The attorney will have to bill more, if he is to be eligible for a bonus at year's end. The awarding of bonuses is routinely a matter of controversy in law firms, as described in Chapter Five on sane compensation systems. Exhausted and misunderstood managing partners and underappreciated, wounded and even vengeful partners are oft-encountered casualties of the bonus wars. Recovery from these psychological wounds can be very long, indeed.

If an attorney fails to make his target for two or three years in a row, his salary will be reduced and, ultimately, he will descend from the status of a partner to that of a special employee, usually called "Of Counsel."

Effects Upon Family Life

Most lawyers adapt themselves while still associates to this unrelenting high level of required production. Too often their families do not. Wreckage in the family lives of attorneys can be quite remarkable, although there is no hard evidence that it is worse generally than that found in the families of other professionals.

As family members fall by the wayside, otherwise skeptical attorneys are persuaded by the mental illness industry to accept new diagnoses with presumed genetic bases. Attorneys accept these new 'illnesses' to avoid facing the fact that they are overworked, that their spouses and children are neglected, and that their resentment is being expressed in illness. It is a bitter irony that people who work so hard to provide for their families should suffer from chronic feelings of failure as spouses and parents.

Obsessive people tend to be judgmental, and this poses a particular problem in dealing with dependent family members. The application of the same unforgiving standards that dominate law firm life to loved ones who want understanding can be alienating and have enduring effects upon the self-esteem of spouses and children.

Women lawyers who attempt to moderate the demands of work with the necessities of childcare are uneasily tolerated within the firm and typically criticized, if only *sotto voce*, for a "lack of commitment."

Indeed, despite the rhetoric of partnership there is very little tolerance for individual problems in law firms. Everyone labors under the same strain and those who complain are called "whiners." Scapegoating and personification as described in Chapter One are common.

Management Challenges

Since a third to a half of the lawyers in a law firm are partners who have been required to purchase a share in the business and are partial owners, the law firm suffers from a superfluidity of incarnate authority; that is, putative managers on the premises who have no one or nothing to manage other than themselves and an associate or two plus a paralegal and a secretary. That they have little responsibility beyond the legal matters to which they attend, does not, as mentioned, keep them from being refractory to being managed themselves.

When the law firm is a Professional Corporation (PC), it is nominally run by a Board, which supervises the election of a managing shareholder. Ordinarily these boards are passive. When they bestir themselves, often enacting group dynamic tensions of which they are largely unaware, they can be dangerous. In Chapter Six, we consider the problematic relations between boards and managers.

Politics

The absence of real lines of authority and accountability above the level of associate in the law firm can make these organizations hotbeds of political intrigue, for nothing much can get done except through coalition building and manipulation.

The law firm is a commercial enterprise not a political entity and the application of political concepts to it is inappropriate. This is true of most organizations. Yet without an understanding of organizational structure, the attorney has no other way of understanding corporate life than by political analogy. Matters that really are ones of divisions of authority and labor are misunderstood in terms of "constituencies," "representation," and "appeals." Inevitably, the reliance upon political conceptions, imagery, and language politicizes the firm and makes it harder to manage. In Chapter Four, we attempt to provide leaders with a conceptual apparatus for understanding, creating, and managing organizational structure.

Attrition and Mentoring

As long as business is good and lawyers continue to do lots of billing at high rates it may seem that nothing much of an organizational nature needs to get done. The financial success of law firms makes them resistant to consultation. Indeed, even in the last severe recession, most law firms remained profitable albeit at a lower rate of increase than has been typical over the preceding several years.

Consultants may seek to stimulate interest by indicating that competitors are better organized. Currently consultants emphasize the necessity of practice group development. Small and medium-sized firms are encouraged to merge in order to be competitive, and guidance for such changes is quite expensive. Yet it is not infrequently the case that the correlation between size and profit among Am Law 100 firms is zero.

Without some tangible reason to collaborate with colleagues, busy lawyers are doubtful about the necessity of group development. It can be inspiriting for a group to come together and get a stronger sense of itself, but without any work that actually requires substantive, ongoing interdependence this proves ephemeral. There are small departments that have as many practice 'groups' as partners.

In reality, 'practice groups' remain largely fictive marketing devices that grace promotional pamphlets while the partner works alone, aided by a legal secretary and an associate or paralegal.

Meanwhile firm-wide problems such as high attrition rates and mentor programs that fail to retain associates receive infrequent, spasmodic attention and too often are left to languish before long. With new lawyers making 125K and often enough considerably more there is little abiding sympathy for their troubles. They leave in droves but are considered "fungible," which they are—at 300K per person in recruitment, training, and lost opportunity costs.

The attempt to create mentor programs is often homegrown and amateurish. When consultants are enlisted, they are frequently untrained in adult developmental psychology and interpersonal relations. They may also lack understanding of the law firm as an enterprise within whose structure the mentoring program will have to be carefully placed and properly led if it is to be effective. We shall have more to say about authentic mentor relationships and the creation of effective mentoring programs in Chapter Two.

The Retiring Generation of Senior Lawyers (58-)

Most law firms contain a stratum of lawyers in the years around 60 who are beginning to think or are actively thinking about retirement. The problem for the individual lawyer is figuring out a viable life structure for old age in which, for the first time in his or her adult life, work will not be at the center, if present at all. How will he or she continue to feel important and useful? The problem for the firm is to enlist the retiring lawyers in moving clients on to younger attorneys and in supporting the efforts of the generation behind them to lead.

The problem for management is that these senior attorneys have large books of business and in other ways retain considerable authority, even after they have relinquished formal leadership roles.

In Chapter Seven, we discuss the particular concerns of the three generations of which the law firm and other organizations typically consist: *The Entering Generation* (23-40), *the Leadership Generation* (40-58), and *the Retiring Generation* (58-).

Helping Attorneys

Lawyers do not go to law school to learn to be department heads and managing partners, any more than physicians train to become heads of hospitals or professors deans. It's a good thing, since professional school offers no guidance in this. When a professional person enters a management position, he or she does so without benefit of training and often of relevant experience.

In the pages that follow, there may be moments when attorneys feel that I am laughing at them. I am. I am also laughing at myself and at all of us caught in a crucible of responsibility and ignorance, as most professional people are who take management roles. My hope is that lawyers will be able to laugh with me. Perspective rather than self-blame is needed and a bit of humor can help provide it. After all, we come by our incompetence honestly.

At the turn of the last century, some 20% of workers in the Western countries were employed in formal work organizations. Most worked at home, in cottage industries, or small family businesses. The percentage now is 80. With the greater size of enterprises, greater complexity occurs. Their structure and dynamics are no longer understandable on the model of the family, the only group that most of us begin to understand. At the same time, the formal work organization is different from the crowd or a political entity like the nation state—other collective forms about which there is a longer tradition of analysis and conception.

From an historical perspective, the modern organization is new and as such not well understood. As noted, the most sophisticated attempts at understanding are now only about 50 years old. By contrast, we have over 100 years of serious theorizing and disciplined practice in the areas of psychopathology and psychotherapy. We still have much to learn about how to design and lead systems that are both viable in the economy and facilitative of the adult development of workers. This book attempts to move us a step forward in this direction.

A serious obstacle to progress is posed by the culture of blame that dominates many organizations especially ones that are performing poorly. Blame is the morality of the playground and should have little place among serious adults working on difficult tasks. Its primary appeal is to paranoid individuals and moral purists. Of course, there are going to be mistakes; what matters is examining them collaboratively and extracting the maximum learning as a means toward increased competence. The replacement of a *culture of blame* with one of *learning and development* is a major challenge confronting leaders who have the courage and imagination to seek fundamentally better organizations. In these organizations of the future, paranoids and moralists will be out of place and may feel encouraged to get professional help or take other steps required to grow up.

Until we succeed in taking the further steps, marginally competent system performance punctuated by calamitous defaults, and underproductive, stagnating workers with impaired families will continue to be the unnecessary costs of earning a living.

It should be noted that I am also laughing, less kindly, at consultants. I have little hope that consultants will be amused. Unlike lawyers, and other professionals who are actually trained to do their work, the level of relevant education and conceptual sophistication among consultants generally is painfully low.

Freud wrote that leadership—together with childrearing, education, and psychoanalysis—is one of the "impossible professions." Nonetheless, experience has shown that law firm leaders can be helped to make their firms happier, less stressful, and more profitable and to derive genuine professional satisfaction from their roles provided they get competent help. Chapter Three offers analysis and advice for leaders as well as for followers.

Well-trained, carefully chosen consultants brought in before problems become acute crises or chronic debilities can be saving. At all times, a thoughtful reading of the chapters that follow can help attorneys and other professionals lead and participate more knowledgeably in their own lives as well as in the life of their organizations.

Chapter One
Basic Psychology of the Group

1. Personality Types

From time to time, it occurs to the busy, successful attorney that colleagues may not be failed versions of himself, but actually different in some way that could be regarded as other than merely regrettable.

In an effort to deepen the appreciation of these differences, consultants may be brought in to firm retreats to administer personality tests. Typically the tests employed have little demonstrated validity and are interpreted by people who have little or no professional training in test construction and personality assessment. For example, the Myers-Briggs and the Colors tests are popular; they gratify the interest in finding ways to think about oneself that pose no threat to narcissism by suggesting serious flaws.

Although the portraits that these tests draw are far too simple, it can yet be regarded as a step forward if attorneys emerge from the exercise knowing that their partners may see and react to things differently for good reasons. An increased understanding of psychology would help attorneys manage their relations with clients better as well.

Realistic Assessment of Personality

In actuality, psychology in the law firm is more complicated than popular tests can reveal. Motivation and behavior, as well as the meaning of work, are largely determined by an *interaction* of personality type, means of production, generational position, and organizational role. This is true of other organizations as well.

In the law firm, *the modal personality type* is obsessive compulsive, *the means of production* is the billable hour, and *its generational structure* consists of an entering generation of young lawyers (23-40), a leadership generation of attorneys (40-58) and a retiring generation of senior lawyers (58-). Each generation faces different developmental tasks attendant upon its place in the life cycle and each has *different roles in the firm*. These roles are strongly related to generational position.

What, Is Everyone Ill?

It may be startling and unwelcome to see the personalities of people who are not patients described in clinical terms. Am I asserting that all lawyers are ill? To write that obsessive compulsive personality is "modal" within the law firm is to say that this is the type of personality organization that is most frequently encountered; it is not to say that it is universal.

That's the good news; here is the bad: everyone has something.

Just as it is not possible to reach maturity without some sort of physical defect, either constitutional or acquired, it is also not possible to reach adulthood without some kind and degree of personality problem. The vulnerabilities that are inherited or acquired in childhood and adolescence are protected by psychological defense mechanisms that guard against pain but which also prevent healing and obstruct growth. Later experience tends to be selectively interpreted in ways that demonstrate the necessity of these defenses and cement them.

For example, a thoughtful adolescent, who as a child felt that his parents were not as emotionally available as needed, is badly disappointed in love or close friendship. He concludes that he has been sabotaged by his feelings and resolves to be more rational in the future. As an adult, further disappointment will suffice to confirm his belief in the necessity of subordinating feelings to intellect. Ultimately, his attitude toward his own and others feelings may become one of suspicion and even contempt.

Each of us has obsessive compulsive trends in his personality and no more so those who go to law school. Personalities of this type are common among all successful professionals—medical, academic, technical, and others. Indeed, some measure of obsessive compulsiveness is required to live in complex, technical modern societies. One needs to be able to read the nutritional table small print on the cereal box carefully in order to get safely from breakfast to dinner.

Whether we should consider ourselves sick or not is a matter of severity—and perspective. As the epidemiologist replied when asked how her husband was, "Compared with what?"

Obsessive compulsiveness is reinforced in the lawyer's personality by the highly technical nature of most legal work, the rapid production that is required, and because the costs of the work and of error are so great.

Defining Personality Characteristics

The defining characteristics of obsessive compulsive personality are hyper-rationality and fear of emotion; judgmentalism; self-control (which extends to a need to control others); preoccupation with fairness and balance (which defends against underlying concerns about aggression); rigidity; and, a preoccupation with detail to the exclusion of context.

The inability to see contexts becomes an important liability in understanding other people or performing high-level management and leadership roles.

A hallmark defense mechanism of the obsessive is reaction formation, the creation of behavior and beliefs that are the opposite of unconscious ones. We describe the operations of this defense mechanism in compensation systems in Chapter Five.

Anyone who has spent time in a law firm knows that lawyers differ one from another. How can this be so, if many have the same basic personality configuration? We can account for some of this greater variability if we add predominant *secondary personality features*. We can then distinguish such significantly different personality types as obsessive compulsive personalities with narcissistic, depressive, manic, schizoid, paranoid or psychopathic secondary features.

Secondary Personality Features

An obsessive compulsive personality with paranoid features is, for example, quite different than one with narcissistic trends. The first is inclined to brood about getting even, the second to withdraw insulted, if not made to feel special. The obsessive compulsive lawyer with manic features feels too important to be troubled by his partners' concerns, the schizoid partner finds relating to others draining and prefers to keep to himself. The self-esteem of the depressive attorney is vulnerable to attacks from himself and others, and he uses work to maintain a fragile sense of self-worth. The obsessive compulsive with psychopathic features is unscrupulous and lacks feeling for others.

Though empathy is typically not the obsessive's long suit, it is quite missing in those few attorneys who have strong psychopathic trends in their personalities.

While obsessiveness and compulsivity go together, their relative predominance varies. An obsessive compulsive personality, *obsessive type,* will be doubtful and indecisive; an obsessive compulsive personality, *compulsive type,* will be driven to act, often repetitiously.

Yet finer differentiation can be gained by adding tertiary personality features; for example, an obsessive compulsive personality, compulsive type, with narcissistic and depressive features.

Severity

As noted, severity is another dimension of personality that matters. There are important differences between an individual with a mildly obsessive compulsive personality and a lawyer with a severe one. The extreme cases are rare. The requirement in most forms of legal work to maintain reasonable relations with clients means that the incidence of debilitating psychopathology among private practice lawyers is low— perhaps ten percent. What we find typically is not debilitated persons but encumbered ones.

In organizations where the professional is kept apart from clients, or protected from them, as in the research university, the incidence of serious personality deformation is higher.

Thus, despite the alacrity with which partners accuse one another of mental illness, at least in private, serious mental illness is not a factor in most law firms—unless, of course, a truly pathological individual succeeds in becoming head of a major department or managing partner of the whole firm. Here the possibilities of general demoralization and even ruin rise worrisomely.

In these instances, the leader is likely to be suffering manic, paranoid, schizoid, or psychopathic personality problems not secondary to obsessive compulsive personality, but as primary personality deformations.

As noted, taking generational position and organizational role—associate, partner, department head, managing partner, senior lawyer—into consideration, accounts for further variety. Imagine an obsessive compulsive male lawyer with depressive features who is a thirty year old associate worrying about making partner. Now make him 50 and head of the corporate department in a recession. Now have him stepping down and facing retirement at 65 uncertain how to form a good enough life structure for old age.

If we also factor in gender and ethnicity, we will have explained most of what can be explained about the behavior of attorneys in law firms. Imagine him a her, then make her a minority member and go through the above roles and generational stages.

Taking Group Psychology Home

Most lawyers adapt themselves while still associates to the unrelenting high level of required production. Too often their families cannot. Wreckage in the family lives of attorneys can be quite remarkable, although there is no conclusive evidence that it is worse generally than that found in the families of physicians and professors. The mental illness industry persuades otherwise skeptical attorneys to embrace new diagnoses with weakly established genetic bases, since these obscure the intractable human problem of overworked and exhausted spouses and parents and reduce guilt. It is a bitter irony that people who work so hard to provide so abundantly should suffer from chronic feelings of irresponsibility and failure as spouses and parents.

The judgmentalism and controllingness of the obsessive attorney can pose a particular problem in dealing with dependent family members. The application of the same unforgiving requirements for order and production that dominate law firm life to loved ones who want sympathetic understanding can be alienating and have long term erosive effects upon self-esteem.

Help for Attorneys

Experience has shown that law firms can be made happier, less stressful, and more profitable provided firms get competent help. Associates can be coached to manage their relations with supervisors more effectively. Partners can be taught to be better mentors. Department heads and managing partners can be helped to lead more effectively, and retiring partners can be aided in their attempts to let work go and transition their practices. Referrals to competent clinicians for attorneys who need and want psychotherapy can be made. But here, as in choosing other experts, help must be carefully sought. Lawyers need to proceed with the same critical diligence as in the choice of an architect, a tax and estate advisor, or a physician.

It is necessary to inquire fully into the consultant's credentials, training and experience. A master's degree in 'coaching' from a diploma mill, let alone weekend workshops, will not suffice. Lots of experience built upon a weak conceptual foundation yields the same kind of effectiveness that physicians had in 1800 before medicine became scientific. What is wanted are consultants who are fully trained psychologically and expert about the law firm. There are not so many of these.

Attorneys should recall how little they knew after three years of law school and consider how many more years were required before genuine competence was acquired. A deeper understanding of the complexities of their colleagues' psychology helps attorneys recognize that the matters they entrust to consultants are not simpler than the legal matters that challenge them.

2. Human Nature: The Case of Robert

Robert is an advanced associate in litigation with a talent for marketing. Extroverted, charming and quick-witted, his success in gaining new clients has cast a shadow over his advancement to partnership. Senior partners complain about selfishness, junior partners about client theft. Incidents of apparently happy clients switching to Robert have achieved the status of legend within the firm.

One day Robert is offered an appointment to a prestigious business association board, one that would plug him into the community at a high level of political influence and wealth. Enhanced opportunities for him and his firm would seem to abound. Delighted, he tells the executive director, Edward, with whom he has a friendly relationship. Edward congratulates him enthusiastically. That same day, Robert tells Steven, head of the litigation department, who urges him to accept the offer.

One week later the managing partner learns about Robert's appointment in the newspaper. He is furious. "There he goes again, putting himself ahead of the firm. It's always about Robert with him!"

Faulty Structure or Deviant Personality?

Surely the managing partner has a point. A seat on a board of this importance positions the firm in certain ways in relation to existing clients and future ones. It constitutes *de facto* an intervention in the community that has implications for the firm as a whole. The relationship between the firm and its marketplace is the special province of the managing partner and changes in it should not be made without his knowledge.

Wasn't this an example of Robert trying to one up his doubting partners and finesse them on the question of advancement to partnership? And wasn't it rudely impolitic to put the managing partner in a position where he is among the last to know of his firm's success?

Let's take a closer look.

To whom does Robert report? The idea of "reporting" is somewhat foreign to the law firm, as it tends to be in professional service organizations generally, and is certainly not appropriate between partners. But this firm, like many others now, consists of departments and or practice groups each of which has a head. It also has an executive committee of which the executive director is a member; the executive director, Edward, was the first person Robert told.

It could be said that in telling him, Robert was informing the committee, since Edward would surely report the news or, acting on the committee's behalf, advise Robert to wait before accepting the invitation.

Edward did neither of these things because, like many executive directors, the fact that he is on the executive committee does not change the reality of his position, which is that of head of administration. He is a "non-lawyer" and has little authority in relation to attorneys, and they do not report to him.

Law firms typically have a hybrid organizational structure with a traditional system of authority and accountability for administration and a much looser one for lawyers. Placing the executive director on the executive committee creates a basis for greater integration between the two sectors but does not insure it.

Relation of Department Heads and Executive Committee

In the structure that exists, Robert reports to his department head, Steven. He is a subordinate member of Steven's department and no other. And, in fact, he told him of the offer promptly, and Steven advised him to accept it.

In most businesses, this would be the end of the story. Robert has told his supervisor about the possibility of doing something that has firm-wide significance, and Steven has told him to go ahead.

Why didn't Steven tell the managing partner? Because in this firm department heads do not report to the managing partner; there is in fact no structural connection—no line of authority and accountability—between the two positions. Steven is not a member of the executive committee, despite being a department head. Along with all other senior partners, he is a member of an advisory committee, which has no formal authority or specific responsibilities. It is supposed to meet regularly but does not.

It is also true that, like many senior partners, Steven is something of a law unto himself within the firm. His seniority, accomplishments, book of business together with his age disincline him to report to anyone and those who are in some measure superordinate to him, like the managing partner, are uneasy about trying to direct him.

Isn't Organizational Structure Too Boring?

Many people find considerations of organizational structure formalistic and boring, but, like physics, it is about the way things work. When structure fails, individuals get blamed.

Most people are only dimly aware of the structure within which they work, and in law firms it tends to be rather murky. Personality on the other hand is visible in all its glory, and it is emotionally satisfying to blame people. Blaming comes naturally to highly trained faultfinders, and it allows for the discharge of the irritation that accumulates from long-term efforts to compete with and get along with others. Thinking in terms of structure has only the satisfaction of clearer understanding and the enhanced competence in one's organizational role that comes with it.

The evolution of law firms from professional associations to complex businesses has resulted in greater differentiation of organizational structure, but this has often been done with little competent guidance, imperfect understanding, and much ambivalence. We will offer some clarity and advice on structure and its management in Chapter Four.

Within a structure that offers scant clarity about the reporting obligations of one's role, the mature collaborative aspects of persons are underutilized, even frustrated. Worse, bad arrangements—bonus-laden compensation systems is an example we will consider later—bring out the worst in people.

As I shall describe in greater detail, accomplished attorneys are reduced to the level of greedy and vengeful children by the sugar plum prospect of juicy bonuses and the reality of the more modest ones actually awarded. Their behavior is attributed to human nature though it is in reality sociogenic—organization caused.

In fact, human nature has many sides. What is needed are structural arrangements that bring out the best in people. In the case at hand, weak and missing links in the structure led to the perception of bad behavior and bad character in a promising associate.

3. Scapegoating: The Case of Gridlock and Stasis, LLP

Many people, including attorneys, believe that lawyers have difficult personalities and that within the law firm dwell partners who can be likened to the viper, the 800-pound gorilla, and the preening flamingo.

Since these creatures are impervious to human influence, it is thought inconceivable that their treachery, belligerence, and narcissism might be a symptom of organizational dysfunction.

Is it possible that such problematic behavior originates not in the personality of the difficult person, but rather in unresolved disagreements about firm direction, poorly designed and managed organizational structure, and inchoate concerns about the marketplace?

Compared with such colorful characters, firm goals and organizational structure seem hazy, invisible, or immaterial. Unpleasantness at work is felt personally, and since each of us is a brilliant diagnostician of the character pathology of others, we tend reflexively to attribute organizational problems to individuals. Pressed between demanding clients and hefty billable hour obligations, partners' frustrations with colleagues accrue and fester until the idea of punishment, even exclusion, becomes an alluring expedient.

Josef Stalin liked this approach to system dysfunction and expressed its central tenet succinctly: "No man, no problem."

Personification and Scapegoating

I call the attribution of group matters to individuals "personification." Personification lies at the beginning of a continuum that ends in scapegoating. Efforts to solve organizational problems at the individual level tend to be ineffective, since one is treating the symptom rather than the illness. When the individual is primarily acting out group problems, after his exclusion, the problem remains with the group, and, before long, another scapegoat will have to be found.

Worse, it can be damaging to the "problem" individual. To be singled out so negatively can injure a person's self-esteem, reputation and career.

12

It can also be self-fulfilling as group pressures induce the scapegoat to act in deviant ways, if only through rigid expectations in which questionable behavior is cast in the same negative light and other kinds of behavior are ignored.

The well thought through removal of an individual from a group is sometimes necessary. There *are* individuals whose personalities are so problematic that they poison organizational life. A malignantly aggressive, paranoid person can destroy a group and a psychopath can do great damage before he or she is finally faced down and expelled.

There are attorneys who, even with less obvious concerns, *do* need psychotherapy. And, there are many attorneys who have trouble negotiating normal transitions in the life cycle and in their careers. Problems with balancing work and family life among junior partners, troubles senior partners have in stepping aside and allowing younger partners to lead, and anxieties about retirement among the old are common and profit from coaching. We shall have more to say about problems specific to the generations in Chapter Seven.

Even if they do not create them, persons with vulnerable personalities or those going through life and career crises may over-react to organizational problems and make them worse. Firm leaders can take the pressure off resonant individuals by shifting the focus from them to firm-wide dilemmas and challenges.

Elliot, A Flamingo

Recently I was asked for help by an old firm that was being "wrecked by a greedy partner." Elliot, a flamingo in the zoology of the law firm, was valued for his contingency case successes but resented for his repeated demands for more money. Although he managed to keep a number of associates busy, he did not himself routinely log long hours. When he had a big trial, he worked hard. When he had little to do, he did little and was unapologetic about it. At one of these times—and this incident had achieved the status of myth within the firm—he had been seen through open door sitting with his feet upon his desk, flicking playing cards into a waste paper basket.

The old guard of Gridlock and Stasis worked increasingly hard in a practice where hourly rates were declining. They saw Elliot's behavior as a mockery of their values and an augury of a day when they would become obsolete and the flamingos triumphant. Yet these senior partners would neither assume leadership openly nor allow anyone else to lead. Since they represented the firm's tradition of diligent toil, their moral influence within the firm remained great and little could be done without them.

Though the old guard had put up a younger partner to "administer" (sic) the firm, she had no book of business and little influence.

For his part, Elliot did not understand that by asking for more money, he was really dramatizing the counterfeit leadership of the firm. In so flagrantly flouting the group's traditional culture, he was challenging the managing partner to do something about it and demonstrating the passive irresponsibility of the firm's real leaders.

The firm was paralyzed by an inert, unacknowledged struggle over direction and leadership, issues that pressed because of worrisome changes in the firm's traditional practice area. These questions made everyone so anxious that they could neither be thought about clearly nor talked about explicitly. Instead group discussion stayed obsessively focused upon the concrete and illusorily rational level of Elliot's compensation.

Questions Managers Need Answered

Many law firms, like Gridlock and Stasis, are simply existing rather than being actively led. Managing partners and other firm leaders need to consider the possibility that underlying the problematic behavior of one individual or subset of individuals reside firm-wide worries about leadership and direction. They need to think less about individuals and more about the nature of their firms—i.e., their tasks, leadership, structure and marketplace:

- Has a future direction been clearly identified?
- Has this vision been compellingly communicated to others?
- Do other firm leaders embrace this direction; if not, how can a leadership coalition be formed to support it?
- How can a new vision of the future be pursued without destroying the firm's traditional culture?

When goals are poorly defined and their respective priority obscure, groups tend to elevate methods to the status of goals without knowing they are doing so. This is especially likely to occur when people feel anxious and inadequately led. "The way we do things around here" becomes more important than the results achieved. Pressure shifts from achievement to conformity. The situation becomes ripe for personification and scapegoating. I call this phenomenon "task displacement," and my research shows that it is surprisingly common in professional service organizations.

Unfortunately, at Gridlock and Stasis the process of scapegoating was so advanced by the time I was called in that there was little I could do but identify it and warn of its likely consequences. Sure enough, Elliot soon left, taking several of the best associates with him. One by one, other partners followed. The dwindling group of old guard lawyers attributed the leaving of each partner to character failings, and there was much bad feeling, recrimination and repeated threats of lawsuits.

More timely intervention would have helped the group to stop personalizing the problem, understand the challenges it faced in a changing legal marketplace, and make rational choices with regard to future directions and requisite leadership.

As in seeing an internist, when it comes to consultants, it's better to call too early than too late.

4. Stress Management: The Case of the Toxic Office

Unrelenting stress is a fact of life in the modern law firm. From first year associate to managing partner, the twin demons of speed and perfectionism bedevil. Lawyers are under pressure from clients for faster, cheaper results, as well as from their firms for greater productivity. The convenience and speed of communications technology, while making life easier in some respects, in others adds to our burdens by giving us more to respond to coupled with the expectation of faster response. Meanwhile, families fail to applaud the sacrifices at work and instead press their own unmet demands.

Life is not much easier on the administrative side of the firm. Relieved of the abrasions of client pressure, staff are met with the exigent demands of lawyers, each of whom regards himself as their employer. In this view, the lawyer has a productive role, since he brings in money, while the staff member merely costs it and must justify his existence by making it easier for the attorney to get work out and bill for it.

The administrative side of the firm tends to be more structured than the legal side because of the diversity and interdependence of its roles and its responsibility for billing and expense management. The structure should serve to protect the individual staff member from the depredations of direct subordination to multiple attorneys. If an attorney wants a check cut, he may not go to any bookkeeper but must rather go to the head of accounting or, in a larger firm, to the executive director.

The position of executive director has proliferated over the past twenty years, as the increasing size of law firms has required a more articulated organizational structure. The executive director has the task of teaching lawyers that, regarding administrative matters, they had best come to him rather than to members of his staff and, on matters of firm-wide significance, to the managing partner. Managing partners who understand the value of executive directors support the structure even as few resist entirely the siren call of micromanagement.

"Everything Would Be Ok, If People Would Just Grow Up and Stop Complaining."

While the stressful nature of law firm life is widely recognized, costs to the individual and the firm of the chronic stress are not. As billable hour obligations increase and the number of hours in the day do not, and while it can be shown that the attorney is spending more of his waking life at work than at home, partners who complain too loudly are considered weak or childish. For an associate to complain would be disqualifying, for a staff member, a moral failing.

The Case of The Toxic Office

A mid-sized, full service firm in Los Angeles opened a satellite office in Orange County, primarily because one of the founding partners had a vacation home there to which he planned to repair for semi-retirement. As it happened, this partner had no intention of taking on the administrative responsibilities of opening and running a new office and instead the burden fell to a junior partner with clients in Orange County. The junior partner brought with him an advanced associate.

Within a year, the junior partner had succumbed to a virulent disease. Not long after that, the associate left with a host of health problems. Over the next several years, one secretary after another left the new office, most bowed by physical afflictions. Meanwhile the founding partner continued his occasional visits to the Orange County office from which he lunched fabulously with wealthy clients. When his digestion was disturbed by the sight of another staff member being helped from the office, he would express dismay and call the executive director in Los Angeles demanding that something be done.

The executive director had 25 secretaries, including the few in Orange County, for whose assignment, workflow and general supervision she was responsible. She was also responsible for a small staff of bookkeepers, information technology and office premises people. In her spare time, she also took care of human resource issues. Her own background was in accounting and generally the management of those matters was unproblematic. She was also fortunate in having IT and office premises workers who were competent and responsible.

Over time, the executive director too became wearied of her responsibilities and afflicted by health problems that appeared stress related. She suffered from neck and back pain and fatigue for which she sought relief in anti-inflammatory drugs, yoga, and counseling. While each of these was temporarily palliative, the discomfort grew.

Could she, she asked the managing partner, have an hour or two of an organizational psychologist's time to help learn how to manage the stress? Though clearly not pleased at this unanticipated expense, the managing partner agreed. The executive director was made to feel that if relief were not soon in coming, continued complaint would be unwelcome.

Working Relationships Not Vertebra

It did not take long to discover the nodal points of the stress. They were organizational not vertebral.

The problem concerned the large number of secretaries for whom the executive director was responsible and their working relationships with attorneys. When these pairings went well, the secretaries became refractory to administrative supervision, accepting the authority only of the partners to whom they were assigned. When they went poorly, the secretaries became nonperforming or ill. Sometimes they quit. Especially in the Orange County Office, the executive director typically heard about the difficulties far too late to intervene effectively.

Stress Reduction

What help did the executive director have to handle so many direct reports? She had a workflow coordinator for the secretaries. The existence of this potential number two position provided a structural basis for relief of some of the stress on the executive director. But in fact it served only as a nodal point. Why? Because instead of developing a good working relationship with the work flow coordinator, delegating to her substantial responsibility and authority vis- a- vis the secretaries, the executive director engaged in boomerang delegations, where, at the first inkling of delay or insufficiency, she would recover the delegation and do the job herself. This had the self-fulfilling consequence of rendering the workflow coordinator less competent than she would otherwise have been and diminishing her usefulness to the executive director.

An enduring reduction of the executive director's stress would result from a better supervisory relationship with her No. 2, the workflow coordinator.

There was another nodal point. Where one was located immediately below the executive director, this one was located directly above. The executive director had a weekly supervisory meeting with the managing partner. The meeting was used largely for information sharing. The managing partner told the executive director of firm-wide matters that she would need to be apprised of to do her job.

For her part, the executive director told the managing partner of her plans and procedures regarding staff. Often, when the executive director had the floor, the managing partner read her emails or glanced at her cell phone. When the executive director began to talk about a management problem she was having with a secretary, the managing partner indicated impatiently that the executive director should demand that the secretary shape up. The managing partner offered no help—nor perhaps did he have any to offer—on the level of a joint examination of problems and a continuing exploration of how best to deal with them.

An enduring reduction of the executive director's stress would result from a better supervisory relationship with the managing partner.

Each relationship, the managing partner-executive director and the executive director-work flow coordinator, needed coaching. How would that be done? As an effective minimum, one meeting a week with the managing partner and one with the executive director for some six months could serve.

What would that cost? Compared with the recruitment-training-severance-recruitment costs of replacing secretaries and the potential cost of replacing the executive director, very little. Helping the managing partner and the executive director to become better supervisors would constitute what the economists call *an investment in plant,* strengthening the firm's management capacity with radiating effects extending well beyond the stressed individual.

5. Problem Drinking and Loss Prevention: The Case of Guppy

Gridley was worried. He and Guppy had been partners in the merger & acquisitions group for many years, and now an associate had told him that Guppy smelled of alcohol and had rambled the night before during a conference call with clients. Another associate complained that Guppy was hard to reach. Gridley received these reports with appreciation and promised confidentiality. As practice group leader, he felt he had to encourage surveillance.

Gridley phoned Carboy, the department head, who was also general counsel. Carboy, too, had had a friendly relationship with Guppy, though it had recently been strained by a bonus dispute. The dispute involved Guppy's hours, which had been down two years running. Firm management had leaned heavily upon him to pick up his pace. The previous year, reaping the success of earlier marketing efforts, Guppy had billed a truly prodigious number of hours and was continuing to do so. Despite this extraordinary recovery, his bonus had failed to keep pace. In a highly elaborate and personalized compensation procedure, the managing partner had gathered data from the department head, practice group leader and fellow practice group partners. He had also gathered data and conducted interviews with Guppy. After long conjuring with the quantitative and qualitative data, the managing partner awarded Guppy a bonus that was 25K less than Guppy thought it should be. This deliberation had taken two months.

Wounded and outraged, Guppy mounted an appeal based upon a review of other bonus awards, that year and recent, relative productivity data and historical curves. This took a month. After a careful review of the appeal data and lengthy consultation among firm management, Guppy' appeal was, with sweeping counter-argument and an appeal to patience, denied. Guppy was stunned. How could his friends treat him this way?

He resolved to encourage inquiries from headhunters and continued his prodigious labors with an eye toward revenge.

A Dramatic Intervention Forestalled

After consulting with the general counsel, Gridley spoke with Guppy's former mentor, Chesney Wold, who had also previously had a friendly relationship with Guppy but who had since grown peckish towards him for neglect. Wold was famous for phoning his protégés at home to conduct lengthy consultations on joint matters but once Guppy had outgrown the mentor relationship, he had left off answering the phone himself and set his family upon standing orders, should Wold call, to tell him that he was out.

Wold asked to meet with me. When I arrived, the firm's lone founder, Smallweed, was in attendance, too. Wold laid out the data described above, although without mention of the productivity-bonus contretemps. He added that, having always been skinny, Guppy seemed recently to have grown a paunch.

For Smallweed the data were conclusive. He himself was a recovering alcoholic and he knew one when he saw one; Guppy was in denial and an intervention was needed. I asked if there had been complaints from clients or any reason to think that his legal work was impaired. There were none. I said that I could believe that the data they had observed constituted problem drinking and the need for help, but that I could just as well imagine they did not. Smallweed grew impatient and, declaring himself a "man of action," pressed the need for intervention. I noted that springing an intervention on Guppy would likely make him very angry and might alienate him from his associates, partners, and firm. It was, I warned, a step to be taken only upon sound evidence and an absence of workable alternatives.

Subsequently I learned that years earlier Smallweed himself had been dragged off the premises by well-meaning family, colleagues and friends and clapped into an inpatient facility. It had taken some time for the founder to come around to recommending that the experience be provided to others.

Perhaps two weeks had now gone by during which numerous conversations had gone on among associates, practice group leader, general counsel, senior partner, founder and consultant regarding Guppy.

But something had yet to occur that needed to. What was it?

No one had spoken to Guppy about the drinking question.

Avoiding The Problem

Who should have? Gridley, because he is closest to him at the lowest relevant level of authority. Why should this matter? Because each step up the authority hierarchy raises the stakes, loads the interaction, and provokes defensiveness. When should he have initiated this conversation? Immediately, with the hope of involving as few people as possible and of preserving uncontaminated, Guppy's working relations with others. Should Gridley emerge unreassured from his conversation with Guppy, he could then involve the general counsel and perhaps a consultant. Even better, Gridley could follow up quickly with a second conversation restating his concern, and a third and then, if concern remained, bring in others.

Alcohol and Risk

Problem drinking among partners is no laughing matter. Among lawyers, more than half of all discipline and malpractice claims involve some form of substance abuse, as do most trust fund cases. Some readers will have noticed that several of the pseudonyms above are taken from Dickens' *Bleak House*, his great novel about an endless inheritance litigation. The names are meant to amuse but have no special suitability to the actual people involved. The attempts at humor do not concern the drinking but the extraordinary difficulty partners have in talking to each other about problems. Skilled in conflict against opposing counsel, partners can be shrinking violets with each other.

This exaggerated delicacy promotes secrecy and creates a paranoiagenic work environment.

Consumption Data

By historical and cross-cultural standards, Americans do not drink very much. US alcohol consumption is 40th in the world. We consume about half that of most European countries, and the historical trend in US drinking is downward. In the individual case, drinking tends to decline with age.

Diagnosis

Over half of American adults drink regularly, several times a week or daily. Normal drinkers comprise the majority of these people; they drink in moderate and controlled ways that rarely lead to drunkenness and do not interfere with the performance of work and family roles. For many, it is a civilized social pleasure that is part of the dinner ritual. It does not lead to increased alcohol consumption over time.

Problem drinkers constitute perhaps ten percent of adults who drink. Some estimates place this number higher among lawyers and reason that this results from the unrelentingly stressful nature of much legal work. By problem drinkers, I refer to people whose drinking interferes significantly with health and work and family functioning, and which leads to dangerous behavior such as drinking and driving and or binge drinking and disappearance from work and family.

Some problem drinkers will desist following a dramatic episode. Others, and this turned out to be the case with Guppy, increase their drinking in response to increased stress. When the stress diminishes, so does the drinking. Indeed, Guppy's partners may have recognized unconsciously that the pressure they had placed upon him for increased productivity was a major factor in his overdrinking. This sort of unconscious guilt leads people to treat problems indirectly, as though they feared that a simple, direct inquiry would lead Guppy to declare, "I am killing myself to meet your demands and now you complain that I am drinking too much?"

Some problem drinkers will progress to full blown alcoholism, some will retain the same level of problematic drinking throughout their lives.

Alcoholics constitute perhaps another ten percent of people who drink. An alcoholic cannot get through a day without alcohol, when deprived of it will go to extreme lengths to get it, and hides his drinking from others.

The percentage of the population that drinks too heavily is stable. This suggests that there is a subset of drinkers who should not drink, perhaps with genetic predisposition to excess, perhaps in association with other genetically predisposed mental illness such as bi-polar disorder.

Effective Intervention

Taking problem drinkers and alcoholics together, some twenty percent of regular drinkers need professional assistance. Psychotherapy can help problem drinkers moderate their consumption. The chances of helping a practicing alcoholic in this way are poor. Once he or she has become sober, psychotherapy can support abstinence by working through the personal problems that threaten it.

In Guppy's case, the direct, friendly confrontation of the practice group leader, better delayed than never, did the trick for the moment as did ultimately the successful conclusion of the very large deal and its associated pressures that Guppy had been working on. In addition, I was able to recommend to Guppy better methods of stress management, some of which he adopted.

Whatever had been the level of Guppy's drinking before, it had never come to the attention of his partners. That it had done so now meant that it had increased in response to something—the demand that slackened productivity be dramatically raised. What was needed was not a cure for Guppy's drinking—on his own time, that was his business—but a return to a level of functioning that kept it out of the workplace. Gridley's direct and concerned one-on-one intervention was sufficient to make Guppy realize that his drinking behavior had to be curbed. It also provided a basis for subsequent interventions, should they be necessary.

Solving The Mystery of Partner Behavior

Too frequently, I have the following conversation with managing partners:

Managing partner: "Throckmorton is doing X."

Consultant: "Why is he doing that?"

Managing partner, exasperatedly: "*I* don't know!"

Consultant: "Have you asked him?"

6. The Process of Entry: The Case of Kafka and Franz, LLP

Lawyers are familiar with thinking in terms of organizational processes when it comes to matters such as making partner. They understand that this is not simply a discrete event but an individual-firm process that occurs over time and has a beginning, a middle, and an end.

Attorneys are less aware of another system process, that of *organizational entry*, although they work amongst its effects every day. As a phenomenon, organizational entry is not particular to law firms, but occurs in various industries. In law firms, it most commonly involves the bringing in of new associates and lateral partners.

In both cases, the process of entry takes a matter of years, not months, typically two or three but sometimes more. For example, it is in years two and three that most associates are lost. The manner in which the entry takes place has enduring effects upon the individual's mode of participation in the firm. In some cases, it operates as a silent determinant of precipitous departure; in others, of meaning and behavior decades after entry.

In the case of a lateral partner, which is the one that will concern us here, the individual needs help in becoming attached to the few people who will be most important to his or her sense of belonging to the new firm. These key individuals are usually ones in leadership roles; the most senior lawyers who might serve as mentors, practice group leaders or department heads, and managing partners. When the process goes well, the newcomer feels that he is accepted and has joined a good group. When it does not, the newcomer remains on the margin, a critical and criticized outsider. The latter state of affairs can characterize a lateral's entire career with a firm or, as noted, it can lead to departures.

During the early part of the entry process, perceptions of both lateral and firm are unstable and vulnerable to distortion. Though each has selected the other, there is an inevitable mixture of hope, fear and ambivalence attendant upon the choice. It does not take much to tip the balance of ambivalence from positive to negative and for exaggerated negative perceptions to harden into psychological realities.

The Case of Kafka and Franz, LLP

Kafka and Franz, LLP is a mid-sized Denver firm offering patent and trademark services with secondary practices in litigation and employment law. As typically occurs, their most successful lawyers headed its practice areas. These now facing retirement, a younger cadre of attorneys in their 40s and early 50s was now taking over the primary leadership roles, including that of managing partner.

For the past seven years, patent and trademark had been king and the litigation group had languished. Indeed, this small group of attorneys had come to be seen as a dysfunctional unit within the firm. Havisham, a senior lawyer and head of the practice group renown for her courtroom brilliance was often out of the office and even those partners diligently in attendance were typically 25% below their billable hour targets.

Tired of trying to lead a group of individuals that seemed inert, Havisham urged the managing partner to replace her. In due course, this was accomplished and a new, vigorous and younger leader, Grete, took charge.

New Leadership

Grete believed that white-collar crime litigation showed the greatest potential for growth. Over the years, they had had to refer out several of these high profile clients. This was her area, and the group had a talented young associate who also aspired to this kind of work. Grete believed that if they could recruit a junior partner with relevant experience, a critical mass would be formed from which growth would emanate.

The litigation group had a checkered history integrating laterals and the managing partner was initially skeptical. Ultimately, Grete convinced him and Samsa, a lateral junior partner from a San Francisco firm, was successfully recruited. This was quite a coup as Samsa showed great promise as a young litigator and was well liked by his former colleagues. For his part, Samsa had heard of Havisham and was anxious to learn from her.

An Entering Lateral

Samsa was an immediate hit at K&F. His work was excellent and his billables high. Within eight months, his realization rate was the best in the firm. But before long a strange and malignant transformation seemed to occur. Out of the country and trying to coordinate a client matter with Samsa, Havisham did not hear back from him for two days. Samsa had taken care of the client problem immediately but had not gotten around quickly to reassuring Havisham. On another occasion, Havisham invited him to play tennis with an important client. Samsa did not show up. Although, Samsa had notified the client of his unavailability well in advance, Havisham was outraged. Given to quick and severe judgment, she swore never to work with Samsa again.

Members of the litigation group typically found each other in the halls around five and went out for a drink together. Samsa was never there. People began to feel that he was aloof, unfriendly. Emails sent to him by other partners did not always secure a reply. Working together on a matter, a frantic associate might have trouble finding him. A paralegal reported seeing him early one morning with blood shot eyes. People wondered if he was drinking. Others speculated that he was having an affair.

A Metamorphosis

It was as though the partners had come to work one morning and found that their promising new partner had turned into a beetle.

Discussion of these matters between Grete and Samsa led only to tense but polite, lawyerly disputations. Colleagues rarely asked Samsa how he was getting along and when they did ask, superficial demurrals were readily accepted.

A strange dynamic of exclusion had begun, despite the fact that no one wanted it. Unchecked, this dynamic would drive him out of the firm within a matter of months and, nearly as bad, the firm would learn nothing from it, preferring instead the simple explanation that something was rotten in Samsa.

Meanwhile Samsa was billing 2,100 hours and, despite rumors of client dissatisfaction, his realization remained the highest in the firm. Concerned about what was happening to him, Grete asked me to coach Samsa about problems with work-life balance and communication with partners.

Doing so, I found myself meeting with a friendly and likeable fellow in his late 30s. Far from aloof, he seemed, if anything, needy. As I got to know him, I learned that he was lonely, isolated and nearly swamped by a multifaceted life crisis. One of his children had been diagnosed with a serious disease; his wife was depressed and under the care of a psychiatrist. Having moved to a new area to join the firm, they were cut off from family and friends.

I also learned that he had lost his mentor from the previous firm, who had left one year into their relationship. This departure had been one of the reasons Samsa had been willing to leave. Central among the attractions of K&F had been the opportunity to work with Havisham and in this way, complete his novitiate as a lawyer. Instead he found himself faced with icy, adamantine rejection from his group's senior litigator.

Why hadn't he told Grete about these troubles? Because he was a proud man who felt that he should be able to shoulder problems without giving quarter. Samsa believed that everyone had troubles, and that they should not be used as excuses for lapses from perfection. He also believed that his most important obligations were to his clients and his family. Stretched to his limits, consideration of colleagues came in a distant third. Medical errands consumed his time between work and dinner and, speaking frankly to me, he confessed that he did not like to drink.

Role Performance Arises from Relationships

Too often, lawyers think like psychoanalysts. That is, when a staff member, associate or partner is having trouble at work, lawyers look to some defect in his character or manner of living to account for the problem. This approach has the advantage of letting them off the hook and of justifying their passivity in doing anything about it. The idea that the flawed role performance might stem from problems in working relationships with others in the firm—particularly those with greatest authority—seems unknown.

This "blaming the subordinate" approach isolates and excludes the person having difficulty. The mental illness industry abets this bias by inventing a new diagnosis every year with an assumed genetic basis and an expensive drug with regrettable side effects to treat it.

If Samsa had not lost his mentor, he would have remained with his previous firm and the stable and rewarding network of relations he had there would have supported him during the current crisis. Note that he did not have difficulty with his old colleagues. If in his new firm, Havisham had been willing to complete the mentoring that Samsa needed, he would have settled in more easily, even with the problems in his personal life. After a period of a couple of years, the life crisis that Samsa was suffering would likely have abated one way or another and the entry process been successfully completed.

In hiring me to coach Samsa, the firm was outsourcing mentoring. I welcomed the assignment; first, because Samsa seemed like an outstanding person and second because these misalliances, so common in law firms and so unnecessary, are costly to both firm and person. For the firm, the cost is the several hundred thousand dollars that may be wasted in recruiting, training, and lost opportunities. For the young person, there is a wound to the sense of professional wellbeing and sometimes an inexpungible blight upon career.

A competent coach is good, but Havisham would have been better.

7. Managing Client Relations in Good Times and Bad

Lamenting the near financial collapse of 2008, Economist Alan Greenspan, former Chairman of the Federal Reserve and Ben Bernanke's mentor, admitted that he was "stunned and incredulous that the financial markets and institutions had behaved so irrationally." Stunned and incredulous. Greenspan is a member of a discipline that has held fast to a faith, childlike in its naiveté, in the rational man. Recently, two Yale economists published a wildly acclaimed book that grants a small but ineluctable role to passion (e.g., greed and envy) in economic decision-making. Today with the economy of Europe hanging in the balance, we watch the psychodynamic theatre of an anal retentive "rules are rules" German leader squeezing the life out of a debt delinquent Greek leader.

Who knew? Freud, by contrast, described the relationship of rational Ego to irrational Id as that of a small rider to a large horse. Setting Freud aside, do economists read Shakespeare, study history; did they notice WWI, have they heard about Jonestown? Do they fall in love?

Greenspan's helpless admission is a reminder that the wish that people would behave rationally is just that—a wish; that is to say, irrational.

Faith in Trouble

A managing partner, pooh poohing the recession inspired gloom of his partners, declared with boyish enthusiasm, "people aren't going to stop suing each other!" A ghoulish sentiment? I might have thought so were it not for the fact that recently I was put absolutely in the pink by a call from a former client saying that his company was falling apart and needed my help. I knew I could help him and welcomed the opportunity.

The sun also ariseth, and the sun goeth down, and trouble abideth forever.

Maintaining Communication

Even though lawyers, consultants and others can share the managing partner's confidence in human discord, extra effort may be needed to help with it in a slow economy. Keep in mind that repeat business is easier to get than new business. This then is a time for attorneys to be proactive in responding to their current clients' financial constraints and worries.

If one listens to clients in a sensitive manner, one can hear unspoken concerns about a growing or unpaid bill. Good clients typically feel guilty about payment difficulties and the guilt can lead to an avoidance of contact. You do not want this.

The problem with broken contact is that the silence is filled with negative projections, because people rarely interpret ambiguity positively. Negative projections can occur on both sides and lead to mutual avoidance. When too much time goes by without hearing from a client, one is not likely to think that the silence issues from enduring satisfaction over the last matter completed. Well-trained professionals hold themselves to a high standard and are acutely aware of the imperfections in their own performance. So in the silence, one imagines that a failure to have done more of this or less of that has left the client with a sour residue of dissatisfaction. For the client's part, he or she may be uncomfortable about feeling unable to give you as much work as usual.

It is more important that the relationship endure than that a bill be paid on time. Initiating a sympathetic discussion of the issue, expressing a willingness to help with a new or revised agreement, can lift a heavy weight from the relationship.

A Caveat about Emails

Emails offer a quick and simple way of staying in touch. Yet, as a means of maintaining or reestablishing contact, they can be treacherous. The emailed response "I'm ok," to a question about how one is, can mean either "I'm fine" or "What's it to you?" Over the phone, the meaning could be gotten from the inflection, although the absence of visual cues can also be significant, as one notices when overhearing mindlessly repetitive cell phone conversations. In person, the meaning would be immediately available both by sound and by posture and facial expression.

The vulnerability of the speedy email to misunderstanding is deepened by the expectation of quick response. Here a bit of depth psychology aids understanding and informs action: If it is true that all love issues from self-love, and if it is true that love is the dynamic of connection, then with each email an aquifer of narcissism is sent out into the ether and the sender is, to that extent, diminished. It does not take long for the sender's rosy hope of love returned to wither into resentful rejection. One wants love to beget love. No matter how meager the ability to please, one never takes kindly to its neglect.

An off the clock lunch is better.

Managing Expectations

Professionals of all kinds are typically poor at helping lay clients understand the process involved in the work for which they are contracting. This is as true of attorneys as it is of physicians, organizational psychologists, architects. For G.B. Shaw this resulted from sinister motives. "All professions," he observed, "are conspiracies against the laity." Each adopts an argot, Shaw objected, that prevents clients from understanding what they're doing.

But sinister motives need not be invoked. Professionals work so hard to learn the murky jargon and complicated methods of their disciplines that understandable English begins to seem inadequate. Further, where the task is clear and the methodology at hand, we don't want to talk about it, we want to get on with the work. With more complex tasks, we cannot always explain how we will proceed. We know ourselves to be good swimmers, but how exactly we will get to the other side of a lagoon infested with sharks and menaced by pirates will only be known in the doing. What we are certain of is that if it can be done at all, we are as likely to succeed as anyone else and more likely than most.

Nonetheless, the failure to educate adequately is a common source of client dissatisfaction, because expectations shape evaluation. Expectations are not simply cognitive and conscious but typically involve emotion-laden imaginings. These imaginings are invested with feelings deriving from the part of the personality that remains infused with the hopes and fears of childhood, like Greenspan's expectation of rationality. They occur on the edge of consciousness and may not be fully noticed. If, for example, you tell me that a restaurant is romantic, a fantasy of what it will be like for my friend and me is immediately formed. If the restaurant turns out merely to be pleasant, my friend and I will feel disappointed and be unlikely to return. We will also be less likely to accept your recommendations in the future.

As another example, earlier generations of pediatricians, were taught to perform surprise attack injections on the theory that injections do not really hurt that much and telling children in advance would only alarm them. The result was generations of needle phobic adults. More recently, doctors learned to warn children that they would feel a little prick and most children then accepted the discomfort without strong reaction.

In the absence of understandable information, the client forms hope- or fear-inspired expectations about the steps involved, about what will be required of him, how long it will take, the chances of success and the cost. Getting timely, explicit and substantive information about what to expect allows the adult part of the client's self to prepare for and accept the likelihood of imperfect outcomes and the possibility of bad ones.

Expert-client relationships are dependency relationships and nothing infuriates like unmet dependency needs. Notifying a client about a delay, for example, is far preferable to disappearing. In the later case, reappearing later with a fine work product will only convince your client that you are skilled but unreliable.

Costs

Working at high billable hour rates, it is easy to imagine that a client, even though informed more or less (usually less) explicitly, was displeased by the magnitude of the bill, despite the work having been done competently and the costs documented. Evidence of cost control, such as NC items on a bill, or proactively offered reductions for blemished results or uncontrolled overages can be reassuring. They also diminish obsessive bill scrutiny, since the client comes to feel that he can count on you to help control costs. Large bills are painful to look at, so your preemptive scrutiny frees the client to yield to his own disinclination to do so.

At high hourly rates, the sound of our voices on the phone can set a client's hand to trembling. This is where a cheery salutation that includes the winning phrase "off the clock" calms like a medicine. Off the clock conversations with reticent clients often lead to on the clock work. And even when they don't do so immediately, they keep the relationship alive.

Even the great 2008- recession did not last forever. When the rubble has been removed and the streets cleared, you want all of your relationships with good clients to have remained intact. The rewards of having protected the relationships through the hard times will then be forthcoming, since there is little reason to fear that the return of good times will eliminate trouble.

Chapter Two
Supervisors and Mentors

1. Supervision

I was coaching a partner, Hugh, with whom associates had refused to work. Women and minorities had been especially critical. They complained that he dumped work on them, provided no supervision, then treated their flawed work products with sarcasm and disdain.

Hugh was a very bright man with an infectious laugh. Yet with him, conversation did not flow easily. There were moments when it was hard to think of anything to say; during those breaks in communication, I felt inadequate and imagined that he was judging me. After a time, I learned that he was not feeling critical, he just lacked social grace. In fact, he was quite shy.

Hugh was working with an advanced associate, Edward, who was a minority member. Hugh complained that the man took no initiative and was in danger of not making partner. I told him that minority associates were most vulnerable to feeling isolated and out of place, and that they, especially, needed mentors. I urged him to work more closely with Edward.

In our next meeting Hugh told me that he had given Edward a fresh piece of work but that Edward had failed again to "take the ball and run with it." As we went over the assignment, it became clear that Hugh had handed Edward a task with little indication of what he wanted done, how the task might be approached, nor when the assignment was due. When I asked Hugh why he hadn't been more specific, Hugh said he wanted "to see what Edward would do with it."

Asked to get more involved with Edward, Hugh had set up a test. When Edward failed the test, Hugh recorded the negative results with little comment. It became clear that Hugh equated supervision with evaluation.

Supervision ≠ Evaluation

Supervision is often misunderstood in this way in law firms and other businesses. On both sides of the firm, legal and administrative, superordinate persons act as though being a good supervisor means identifying and correcting error.

Let me offer another definition: Being a good supervisor means creating and managing a relationship in which the likelihood of error is reduced.

Evaluating Instead of Helping

What's the problem with Hugh's approach? Making evaluation primary creates so much distance between associate and partner that communication is impaired and identification frustrated. It also generates a degree of anxiety that—as we know anxiety does beyond a modest level—jumbles thought, shorts memory, and freezes imagination. The priority given evaluation also creates a degree of defensiveness that limits the supervisee's ability to learn from mistakes.

Identifying With the Supervisor

"Identification frustrated," what does that mean? Becoming a partner requires acquiring technical skills, but it involves more than that. It means installing admired, caring partners into one's imagination to be emulated. Associates cannot do that when uncaring, uninvolved partners are savaging their self-esteem. If the associate should manage to survive and prosper, do not ask him to be a mentor, because he may use it as an opportunity to master his own humiliation by humiliating others.

Parents who beat children were usually beaten as children themselves.

Meanwhile law firm attrition rates remain high and the costs of losing an associate are, as noted, around 300K.

Enduring, work-enhancing identifications occur within relationships where criticism takes place against a backdrop of optimism about future mastery.

This cannot be faked. If a supervisor or a putative mentor does not feel confident about the supervisee's potential, he should make certain that the associate works with others who do. If no one does, then a recruiting error has been made and steps need to be taken to keep from turning the firm's problem into the associates.

In its highest form, supervision becomes mentorial and meets the deepest professional needs of the young professional—the need to form a dream of great achievement and have a mentor's help in realizing it.

Good supervision and mentoring are gifts that keep on giving. The properly cared for young come naturally to the proper care of those who follow them. Over time, a firm may evolve where firm-mindedness and genuine collegiality are the rule.

Partners, Too, Can Learn

Does this sound pie in the sky? If none realizes the ideal fully, some firms approximate it far more closely than others, and research shows that they do so through good supervision and mentoring. Partners like Hugh can be taught to be better supervisors and mentors, and mentor programs can be structured and managed effectively, but to do so requires a serious and sustained commitment. It won't do to make episodic, minimal investments in these programs and then when nothing much happens, console oneself with the thought that people don't change: "Hugh will always be Hugh, Edward Edward."

2. Supervisorial Mentoring and Mentorial Supervision: The Case of Throckmorton and Gervaise

Usually with as little thought as possible about the relationship itself, supervision goes on in every organization. Partners supervise the work of associates and some supervisors may be identified as mentors too, yet these roles are different. Those responsible for professional training need to think through clearly the different functions and purposes of these roles, lest training efforts get sabotaged.

The rudimentary functions of a supervisorial relationship are control and evaluation. The supervisor uses his or her authority to monitor the quantity and improve the quality of the supervisee's work. The task of a mentor relationship is different; it is to help the protégé realize his or her potential. This is done not through the direct exercise of authority but by believing in the associate and inspiring the young attorney to do his or her best work.

A supervisory relationship can—and should—have mentorial qualities, just as a mentor relationship often has supervisory ones. A supervisory relationship becomes mentorial to the extent that the issue of evaluation is set aside. A mentorial relationship based upon shared work will have supervisorial aspects.

The important thing is to keep the essential functions of the relationships clear and to act accordingly.

Law firms that fail to provide associates with genuine mentors, separate and apart from their supervisors, may leave associates overly vulnerable to partners' criticism, as the following example illustrates. This is especially the case when the supervision is devoid of mentorial elements.

A Case Example: Throckmorton and Gervaise

I was interviewing the partners of a Montreal law firm as part of a review of their governance structure. As I ordinarily do, I began the interview of one partner, Gervaise, by saying, "My interest is in organizational structure. I am not looking for villains or victims." Gervaise, replied, "There *is* a villain in this firm, and his name is Throckmorton. He is a despicable human being, a cancer on the firm, and I'm not leaving until he's dead!" She then burst into tears.

I stopped taking notes at "despicable" and asked her what had happened. She told me the following story.

Ten years ago, when she was an advanced associate, Throckmorton had asked her to prepare a brief for him. She was flattered and nervous. Throckmorton was one of the firm's top rainmakers, a man widely admired for his important clients and legal accomplishments. Gervaise had never worked with him, and he gave her the file in a rush, with little explanation.

The subject matter was unfamiliar to her. She quickly found that she did not know what she was doing. When she tried to consult with him, he was out of the office. Finally, in desperation, she patched something together and gave it to his secretary with firm instructions to explain to Throckmorton that it was merely a rough draft. This message was not conveyed to Throckmorton.

The following day he flung the document down on Gervaise's desk and said, "This is not at an advanced associate level," and left.

Though 10 years had passed, Gervaise had never gotten over her anger and humiliation. She was so bitter that the firm had attempted on two occasions to mediate the difficulty without success. It was her view that, in the presence of others, Throckmorton simply lied about the event. Later, when I interviewed him, he seemed embarrassed and apologetic.

Poor Delegation

How are we to understand the extraordinary half-life of this episode? Although one could think Gervaise is overreacting, a closer look makes her reaction understandable and predictable. Throckmorton had engaged in a poor piece of delegation; he had not explained to her what was needed nor bothered to make sure that she understood how to proceed. He had not made himself available for consultation as she worked on the piece, and, when she had not surprisingly botched it, he had reacted inappropriately. That being said, although Throckmorton had been insensitive, this was hardly an atrocity.

Performance As a Function of Relationships

It is poorly understood in law firms and elsewhere that work performance is not simply a function of ability and effort but is also strongly influenced by the quality of the relationship in which it occurs. Here, there was little or no relationship between the Throckmorton and Gervaise. In this sort of circumstance, the likelihood of mis- or no-understanding is increased.

The maddening thing for the busy partner is that when he or she has not time to think through a matter, it is precisely this that is needed for the associate to provide competent assistance.

Until a good working relationship is built, it may take nearly as much time to instruct the associate as it would for the partner to do the work alone. One needs to be patient here and understand that educating the associate in this way strengthens the relationship. It is investing in plant, and it will pay off in increased efficiency later.

To understand Gervaise's reaction, we need to understand the extraordinary vulnerability of law firm associates and their need for mentors.

Law schools provide very little training in the practice of law. When law students graduate from law school and enter a law firm, they drop off a cliff. The incompetence of beginning attorneys is nearly complete, and typically their youth adds to the vulnerability. And, because of the importance of the projects and the large size of beginning salaries, the stakes are high.

A hypercritical supervisor doesn't protect the associate from being crushed in the fall; a mentor is needed, or at least a partner whose supervision has mentorial qualities.

Overly critical, uncaring supervisors can become *tormentors*. They threaten self-esteem and morale and are dangerous to internalize.

A good mentor notes errors and corrects them, but sees that these are neither personal nor permanent failings. Again, this takes place in a relationship atmosphere of optimism about future mastery. The mentor helps the associate keep an sustaining vision of competence alive amidst the inevitable welter of mortifying mistakes.

By the time associates get past their third year, they have achieved veteran status among associates and cannot hide, and do not wish to, behind beginner's naiveté.

Gervaise was not a beginner, yet this served only to raise the stakes. She had achieved an initial level of mastery and at sufficient cost that Throckmorton's attack upon it was very painful. For his part, he had simply been in a hurry and had received no help from the advanced associate.

3. Retaining Associates

It is 8 a.m. and I am sitting in the lobby of the main office of a Fortune 300 company. Employees, mostly young, are filing through the security gate moving like characters in the movie, "Night Of The Living Dead," or clerks in the superior court. All are listless; some smile at the few colleagues whom they acknowledge. I report this to the president and chairman of the board and ask him what his attrition rate is. "Probably not as high as it should be," he replied.

How High Should Attrition Rates Be?

Some employees ought to leave. An associate learns over the course of a year or two that he is in the wrong firm or city or profession. Even with the best recruiting, firms will make some wrong choices and select an individual who cannot be helped to fit in productively. Or, an associate who would have done well in a different department, fails to take root in the one assigned. Neither firm nor associate can see this in advance and after a few years of underproductive struggle, the damage may seem irreparable to both. Rather than sharing responsibility, the failure is usually blamed on negative characteristics of the associate.

Attrition is expensive. A conservative rule of thumb is that it costs 18 months of wages to replace a professional person and six months for a clerical one. In the law firm, this would mean an average cost per associate of about 300K. Other estimates specific to law firms place the recruiting-training-lost opportunity-recruiting costs higher.

There are also morale costs more difficult to measure. It is a blow to the morale of a department to have a promising new member decide to leave. It is very hard on the self-esteem of an unproven young lawyer to feel that he cannot succeed in the firm he chose to join, especially if it is his first foray into the world of professional work.

Law firms have been worried about associate attrition for some time. Data gathered by The National Association of Law Placement about the 'Generation Xers' offer little encouragement. Nor is there much reason to be more sanguine about the 'Generation Yers or Millennials.' Of the class of associates taken in any given year, firms lose some eight percent per annum, except in years two and three, when these numbers double. There are increases in magnitude for women and minorities while the shape of the curves is similar.

The average annual attrition rate is about 11%. As such it is not out of line with attrition rates generally among young professional workers, although it is high, for example, compared with very good companies like Microsoft, who also recruit and hire bright, ambitious young people.

It may be that an attrition rate of five percent a year constitutes an irreducible minimum. That would be less than half the national average for law firms and a worthwhile goal.

Why Do Young People Leave?

During the last several years, we heard a great deal of blather about 'Generation Xers.' It was asserted that they are different from previous associates. Yet the label itself is self-nullifying; "X" indicates the identity of the generation to be unknown, but this did not prevent the label from being bandied about freely. Their algebra having long since receded into the mists of time, partners who would not walk about shouting "I do not know what I am saying," enunciated the nullity with solemn conviction.

Often consultants sold it to them. The consultants got it from *People Magazine.*

Similar gibberish has already appeared about the so called 'Millennial Generation' which replaced the briefly exploited 'Generation Yers' and after which momentary escape from the alphabetical progression we will once again be getting to the end of the alphabet. After the 'Zers,' we will then be forced to proceed to its beginning and continue with 'Generation A,' 'B' and so on. It is as though every improvement in cell phones is thought capable of creating a new generation.

The generational appellations have a short shelf life because as members age, they reveal themselves to be very much like the people who preceded them, living similar lives. *Mit den* children, *mit den* mortgages, *mit den* pot bellies, *mit den* boring marriages. The recent exposure of the Canadian dating service for adulterers revealed a near 20% of residents of Ottawa as members. Why so many? A local observer pointed to the simple fact that in Ottawa, people were bored out of their minds. They were living in a city "that fun forgot." How much better is it in Des Moines, Portland, Sacramento, Auckland?

Even as it is widely asserted that the private practice of law has become less satisfying, it is also believed that the departures of today's associates result from weak work ethics. Previous generations of associates, so the story goes, were hardworking, loyal and grateful. They did what they were told and if what they were told included little information about the purpose of an assignment, its nature, scope, methodology, or timeline, they figured it out for themselves.

They were also men.

Mostly. when the average partner of today was an associate, two-thirds of the associates were male.

In reality, the essential character of a generation is given by its place in the life cycle, and the life cycle is a genetic not an historical matter. Thirty-year-olds are not essentially different now than they were in Hamlet's day (he, too, was thirty). At thirty, the individual is roughly half way through the era of early adulthood and faced with the task of reassessing the choices made in the 20s with an eye toward creating a better life for the culmination of the era. That is, he or she is in the age thirty transition (~28-33), and this is where most associates are lost.

Women Associates

The main difference between associates of today and their predecessors is that now half are women. Since seventy percent of partnerships remain male, a gender dynamic is introduced into the authority relationship between partners and associates as groups, and this is truly new. A member of a distinct minority is inclined to keep quiet and try to fit in. When her numbers swell to fifty percent, she is less likely to feel that the problem of fit in the workplace is hers alone.

Many young men are brought up to expect demeaning treatment from other males. They experience it on the playground, from coaches on athletic fields, from upperclassmen in fraternities, from officers in the military, and often enough from older brothers and fathers in their own families. They do not like it but they are led to expect it and even to consider the ability to take it, under some circumstances, masculine.

Emancipated women of the sort that go to US law schools react differently. They have been brought up to expect respectful treatment and to stand up to discourtesy. They do not consider the ability to tolerate abuse feminine. They not only dislike being bullied by men, many will not long accept it. They are insulted and hurt by rudeness, resent it, and believe that this sort of treatment issues from bad values and psychological deformity, not from the demands of practicing law. What self-respecting person, they ask themselves, would accept this sort of treatment?

Partners may wonder: "What is the implication here; are we to coddle associates? How will they stand up to opposing counsel?"

Platoon leaders in the army do not stab and shoot their recruits, they teach them how to do it to others. The best leaders teach in a way that conveys a genuine caring about the novice and this, together with their expertise and accomplishments, evokes admiration and loyalty. It also promotes sustaining identifications.

Women also have, or feel they have, more choices than their male counterparts, including the opportunity to enrich their occupational lives with part-time child care during their 30s. Some men want this option, too, but not as many as the ideology of progress imagines. Law firms have struggled to adapt themselves to the child-rearing wishes of their female associates and when surveyed, nearly all report that they have such part-time policies. A closer look at the numbers shows that almost no one takes this path and of those who do, nearly all are women. My consulting experience with firms reveals that the part-time choice is offered with deep misgivings, even resentment, by partnerships, and is accepted with overriding feelings of personal guilt and professional anxiety by associates.

The law firm as well as technology companies remain male dominated workplaces. The law firm appears to be headed for a demographic train wreck—or, the infusion of better values and more humane practices. Real mentor relationships will hold a central place in those law firms of the future that succeed in retaining talent.

Where Do They Go?

Few law firms conduct exit interviews systematically. Associates who leave tend to be viewed as lazy or disloyal and are disdained. They die a social death the moment they make known their decision to leave. When firms do conduct interviews, they rarely use independent, psychologically sophisticated interviewers. When done in-house, the results obtained are constrained by mutual defensiveness—continuing fears of retaliation on the part of the associate and a faultfinding bias in the interviewer. In this way, a gold mine of valuable information about the firm and its associate development efforts is lost.

If these departed are like others, Gallup research on a very large number of employees in diverse industries identifies problems with supervisors as the primary cause of attrition. The same research identifies twelve factors that characterize highly engaged employees: Eleven of them concern good mentors, supervisors and other developmental opportunities. The twelfth is not compensation.

The specific data about destination that we do have covers about two-thirds of the departed. In decreasing order, they go to other private practice law firms, in-house, public service and—as one combined category—to other professional service firms. Next in the order are solo practice, business, or full-time family or community commitments.

Those who go to other private practice law firms appear to constitute the majority of all departing associates. Further the new firm is often the same size as the old and in the same city.

The implication I draw is that these departing associates were neither lazy nor mercenary, but that a supervisory and mentorial failure occurred in the original firm, a failure that was unnecessary—that is, lacking deep causes in the character of the individual associate or in the ineluctable nature of the law firm. In short, the leaving could have been prevented with modest but informed effort on the part of the partnership, effort concentrated on the first three years when nearly half of the associates depart and where the seeds of later flight are sown. At 300K per departed, what well-led firm would fail to make this effort?

4. Caveat Mentor

The good news is that the call for mentoring is heard everywhere today. That is the bad news, too. The call rises heavenwards in meetings of university faculties, corporate boardrooms, and law firm retreats . Young people should have them and older people should provide them. In law firms, lists of associates are assembled and assigned to partners who are required, like cows in a dairy farm, to enter their stations and provide the goods. But just as farmers know that resentful cows make bad milk and less of it, obliging the middle-aged to serve as mentors to arbitrarily chosen protégés is not likely to set their generative juices flowing.

It has been said that for every problem there is a simple answer and it is wrong. "Mentors for all" may be one of these. Although mentor relationships are certainly very good things, as is true elsewhere in life, even good things can have unintended, sometimes quite negative, consequences.

The trick is to proceed knowingly. To paraphrase H. G. Wells, life is a race between education and catastrophe.

Authentic Mentor Relationships

Mentor relationships are among the few most consequential relationships in adult lives, with effects that can shape entire careers. A well-meaning law firm management committee cannot mandate them. Genuine mentor relationships arise from mutual attraction, shared work and, at best, shared dreams. Trying to create mentor relationships by administrative fiat is like trying to promote morality by placing Gideon bibles in hotel rooms. It may do some good, but probably not much.

Research into mentor-protégé relations indicates that only those who, in the early phases of their careers, had mentors typically reach the highest levels of achievement in various fields of endeavor. More than 50% of all Nobel Laureates in Science had at least one Nobel Prize winner as a mentor. Most of the others had mentors, too. More broadly, two-thirds of the eminent grow up in contact with eminent adults in the field in which they will later excel.

The Mentor's Role

Mentoring has a long tradition. In Homer's *Odyssey*, written some 2,800 years ago, Athena, the Goddess of Wisdom and of War, appeared in the guise of an old villager named Mentor to help young Telemachus begin his journey into adulthood.

Today, the mentor is usually an older person accomplished in the field that the protégé is entering. Ordinarily, he or she has benefited from a mentor relationship and passing the gift along comes naturally. Unfortunately, only about 20% of partners had mentors. The others will need some training and, in some cases, coaching to do so.

What the young adult needs goes beyond advice and opening doors, although these concrete gifts matter, too. The mentor's role is to help the protégé form a dream and bless it. In the case of Telemachus, it was to search for his long-missing father, Odysseus, and help him reclaim his kingdom.

The young attorney's dream may be to become a celebrated litigator, a mediator of Solomon-like judiciousness or a Supreme Court justice.

Alternatively, the dream may be nascent or fragmented, requiring the mentor's help to give it usable shape.

The legal mentor behaves as if to say: "Yes, you can become an outstanding lawyer. I see what is best in you and I know about the world in which you are trying to make your mark. I will help you learn how it is done. With hard work, some luck, and a little help from me, you will get there." This need never be said. It is a palpable aspect of the emotional atmosphere of the relationship—the "vibes," as we say in Berkeley.

Dangers In Mentoring

Because the relationship excites hope, it can also produce great disappointment. A protégé can become masochistically attached to a relentlessly disapproving mentor, internalize him, and suffer long lasting internal attacks upon confidence. I call these negative mentors "tormentors."

More commonly, the protégé comes to resent the former dependence, and the mentor feels unappreciated or betrayed. Typically, by the late 30s the protégé becomes restive and wants free of dependence upon mentors in order to speak with his or her own voice. The protégé has a developmental need for the relationship to end, lest he remain not fully-fledged. The mentor has no such developmental need. The disparity of needs can lead to misunderstanding, hurt feelings, and alienation. Where the two behave wisely—and here the burden of responsibility rests more on the mentor—after a period of separation a mature friendship can develop.

Where the relationship runs against the current of authority, violent rip tides may result. If it works too well, others may try to kill it.

Mentor Relationships Gone Bad

The outcome of an unsuccessful mentor-protégé relationship can have enduring consequences. A successful middle-aged litigator is known for his cynical preoccupation with the corruption and bad motives of others, and he prides himself on his capacity to trick and manipulate people, including colleagues. His associates and most of his peers feel insulted and treated dishonestly but are afraid to confront him. He is the sort of enemy one does not want, for one senses that the war will last a lifetime—indeed there are casualties to which one can point.

What happened? Clearly there are personality problems here, but this is not the whole story. Twenty-five years earlier, when he was an associate, this man had formed a mentor relationship with a senior partner. They quickly grew close, but the relationship ended in bitterness when the mentor took exclusive credit for a high-profile case the associate had brought in and successfully managed without significant supervision. The associate protested, lost, and left the firm, outraged. Now, many years later, the former protégé continues to carry a legacy of resentment that poisons his relations with others. He handles his cases shrewdly and protects his position aggressively, but he has no protégés and it seems that when he retires the only legacy he will leave behind is relief.

Mentoring Against a Flood Current

King Frederick the Great and Voltaire shared a dream of joining genius and political power. As a young prince, Frederick wanted Voltaire to help him with his amateur efforts to write French poetry. Voltaire wanted Frederick's power to supply the myriad rewards warranted by his genius and required by his vanity.

Once Frederick became King, he began to resent his earlier dependence on Voltaire. "When one has sucked the orange, one throws away the skin," Frederick noted, as he attempted to discard his former mentor.

Later, when Voltaire had flagrantly betrayed his protégé-patron's trust, exploited his office, and fled from the royal court in Berlin, Frederick had him arrested. Released, exiled and estranged, Voltaire continued to receive drafts of Frederick's verses. "Does the man expect me," Voltaire groaned, "to go on washing his dirty linen forever?"

It could have been worse.

Envied Mentorial Pair

A richly successful mentor-protégé relationship can arouse explosive envy. One mentoring example caused a major stir in the US and was widely and exhaustively chronicled. Some years ago William Agee, CEO of Bendix, and his protégé, Mary Cunningham, faced questions about their relationship. Cunningham, an MBA, was a gifted executive in addition to being beautiful. Agee brought her up through the ranks at a rate appropriate to her aptitude but neglectful of the feelings of others. After he made her vice president, the uproar within the firm was such that the board asked for her resignation. Before long they asked for his too.

Envious colleagues did not want to believe that their relationship was simply mentorial, although they insisted that no other tie bound them until after they had both left the firm. Controversy about their relationship followed them.

This story reminds us of the fury that can be created by a cross-gender mentorial pair dreaming together among colleagues who may be, by comparison, isolated, stuck and emotionally starved with little to look forward to in work than more of the same.

The Mentor Inside

Mentors are the parents of our adulthood. Our need for them is developmental and in that sense resembles the need a child has for a mother or a father. It is difficult for a young person to negotiate optimally the career and family demands of the adult years without one.

Good mentors live on in our memories and imaginations long after their role has ended. They are an enduring source of strength and inspiration and, in time, we become somewhat like them. In certain challenging professional circumstances, we are guided even decades later by remembering things the mentor did or said. We do not have to look for this guidance, the memories come to mind spontaneously. Since our mentors are usually significantly older, they may also help us age. In the best cases, we have had the opportunity to see how they contrived to grow old without losing their professional vitality.

Mentor-inspired behavior is not divinely inspired and, as we have seen, may not always work. But given the imponderables and high stakes that attorneys and other professionals face, the sense of confidence that comes from working from the inside out can be invaluable. The alternative may be always having to feel that one is inventing oneself.

Choice

The best way to promote genuine mentor relationships is to make them voluntary and worth the mentor's while. The element of mutual interest is essential and substantive work is usually required to join the pair. Maximize choice. Avoid forcing associates and partners into a relationship they do not want and cannot use. The pairings should be evaluated after the first six months, then again at the end of the first year. No-fault reassignments should be available. Partners who are ambivalent should be encouraged to give it a try and resources, such as coaching, made available to help them succeed. Others will take to it naturally and find their working lives enriched.

Homegrown Mentor Programs

Sixty percent of US law firms have "mentoring programs." If you compare their attrition rates with firms that do not have programs, there is no difference. How can this be? Most partners can think of individual cases where an attorney who had had a genuine mentor relationship stays on within the same firm, taking on important leadership and mentoring roles over the course of a long and productive career. And, as consultants, we have seen retention rates improve when mentor relationships are better understood and promoted. Further, we know from numerous studies in diverse industries that mentoring is strongly related to retention.

Nothing for Everyone

A closer look at the data shows that fewer than 20% of firms have used consultants to set up their programs. In the great majority of firms, an attorney is put in charge of designing and monitoring the mentor program. This is like asking a psychologist to draw up your partnership agreement.

In the minority of cases where a consultant is used, an examination of their background suggests that of these 20% only a small fraction is competent. Most have no formal training in adult development and interpersonal relations. Their training in psychology consists in weekend workshops where they learn to sprinkle the latest brand of angel dust, "mentorial circles" being a current example of this sort of ephemera. What knowledge they possess is empirical, based upon having seen this, that, and the other approach attempted. They settle upon the one that generates the fewest complaints, and that requires attorneys to learn little that is new or do anything that is very different.

As one managing partner put it about a lawyer who was running off associates, "Really, all he needs to do is smile when he criticizes them." Really?

If the homegrown mentor program accomplishes little, this can be blamed on the poor work ethic of the "Generation Xers or the Millennials." If the consultant inspired program is ineffective, the untrained consultant has little to fear. Since the press of business soon re-captures the attention of lawyers, firms will rarely evaluate systematically the results of such programs. Should a managing partner demand an accounting for poor results, it can always be shown that the consultant's recommendations were not properly executed. Typically, these recommendations are as ambiguous
 as they are numerous and imperfect implementation can be counted upon.

Put It Anywhere

Even if consultants understood the psychology of mentor relationships their knowledge would be insufficient without an understanding of organizational structure.

Nothing succeeds in a law firm without leadership and no program will long survive that isn't well integrated within the existing firm structure. For example, if the position of Director of Professional Training is created in order to invigorate a firm's mentorial efforts, a change has been made in firm structure. The new role, DPT, will have to be rationalized with those already existing that have partial responsibility for professional development.

It is likely that some of the pre-existing aspects of the structure will have become redundant or unnecessary. This is worse than wasteful of time and effort, precious commodities in bill-by-the-hour law firms. It is worse because the uncoordinated work of multiple role incumbents acts as a constraint upon task performance, since the efforts of one may contradict, or be tangential to, or repeat confusingly, the efforts of another.

Yet, pressed as lawyers are for time, and as skeptical as many are regarding "touchy feely" endeavors, in an astonishing excess of egoism, the attorney who is head of the Caring For Associates Committee, having long complained of the thankless role, will be hurt and resentful when asked to step aside.

In this more complex structure, a thoughtful approach to lines of authority and responsibility will be required and new definitions of a more effective division of labor worked out over time.

Tailor-Made or Off The Rack

Since firms differ in the strength of their practice group, departmental, and top management structures, a mentor program will have to be built differently for different firms. The practice group structure in many firms is little more than a marketing device; these 'groups' are weakly led, rarely meet, and compel little allegiance from their putative members. Burdening practice group leaders with the task of administering a mentor program merely adds the unrealistic to the unreal.

Firms mid-sized and up will need others to implement the DPT's mentor program. In a firm with a functioning departmental structure, under the leadership of the DPT, department heads could administer the effort in their own departments, making assignments, honoring choice, monitoring the progress of each relationship, and making no fault changes where needed.

He or she could alert the DPT to situations in which a consultant is needed to coach attorneys with special problems, such as an underperforming, talented associate or an underperforming, partner mentor. If the department heads formed an executive committee, which included the DPT, under the leadership of a managing partner, monitoring of the mentor program firm-wide could occur consistently. There an eye could be kept on attrition, retention, and the ongoing education and training needs of attorneys. Periodic training meetings to refresh and enhance partners' understanding of mentor relationships and ability to conduct them should be *pro forma*.

To Mentor or Not To Mentor

Supervision must take place in every law firm that has associates and paralegals. The depth of engagement between supervisor and supervisee ranges from glancing, token and superficial to sustained involvement over time in daily work and the creation of work products. Not all firms have the resources to create a mentor program separate from the naturally occurring supervisory one. There are also many firms in which the training and upbringing of associates is not a strong part of their tradition and whose leadership does not really believe in the importance of mentor relationships. In such cases, a firm might be wise simply to focus on improving the generative quality of the supervision it provides.

Generative Supervision

To be generative means to act in such a way as to promote growth. In a supervisory relationship that is generative, performance, as stated earlier, is criticized and error identified in an atmosphere of optimism about future mastery. Performance is criticized but the person is not. Error is confronted as a temporary misstep in an ongoing process of growth to which the supervisor is committed and is confident will continue.

Mentoring is not simply skills training or, in the current argot, the acquiring of a "Skill Set" from Ace Hardware designed for rapid application. Mentor relationships do not so much require extra time as informed effort and a change in firm culture.

Even firms that have the will and resources to create separate mentor programs should work toward making *all* supervision generative; in short, to begin to move away from *a culture of criticism and blame* to *a culture of learning and development*. Firms need to do this, not simply because it is good business to retain talented young workers who become more valuable by the year, but because it is right to do it and wrong not to. Here, too, consultants who combine knowledge of mentor relationships with an understanding of organizational structure and cultural change are needed.

The adult personalities of young attorneys—here, those between ~23 and 40—are still forming. Just as there are critical periods for the development of aptitudes like speech in childhood, such periods exist during the adult years, too. Although individuals can remain amenable to other forms of help, the ability to internalize a mentor ends in the late 30s or early 40s at the latest.

To deny associates genuine mentors is to stunt their growth with consequences that cannot later be remediated. Not only will a significant part of their potential go unrealized, full realization being possible later only when one has had a mentor earlier. It will stock the law firm—yours and the firms they go to and whose refugees become your laterals—with "show me the money" partners whose inability to develop younger attorneys and cooperate with their peers and is all too well known.

Chapter Three
Leader and Followers

1. The Leaderly Manager

Whole forests have been sacrificed for Harvard Business Review articles on leadership. The results have been meager. It is now known that some leaders are above average in height, others below; some are men and others women, some extraverted and others introverted, some loud, others quiet. At the Stanford Business School, it was learned that the only factor distinguishing the leadership of great companies from good ones is persistence. For this sensible result we must be grateful; it, at least, conforms to what we already knew about success in life.

In the absence of the sort of substantive results that could inform action, new terms get coined. Not long ago, we were given "Servant Leadership." Here the idea is that leaders exist to support and facilitate the work of others. This is true enough, since good leaders concern themselves with insuring conditions that facilitate competent work. The problem with this friendly term is that it enables the abuse of authority by obscuring, even pretending to reverse, the reality of subordination. It cloaks in a humility bordering on the Christian the responsibility of managers to evaluate, reward and sometimes punish. It may also distract us from noting the quite extraordinary salaries that are enjoyed by 'servants' in American corporations.

As has been said, even in the ideal conception of the relationship between rider and horse it is far preferable to be the rider. True, a talented equestrian can be said to bring out the best in a horse, but best by whose lights, the horse's or the rider's?

Tasks and Leaders

Leadership is as complex a matter as it is important and the various ways we use the word contributes to its elusive mystique. Sometimes we use it simply to refer to behavior: "After the chair withdrew, Ed led the meeting until a decision was reached." At other times, we use it to describe an enduring quality of a person: "She has leadership ability." As consultants, when we advise firms that they need leadership, it is not always clear whether we are referring to a person who would be willing to accept the leadership demands of a management role, or one who is eager to inspire and direct others.

We shall not get very far in our attempts to understand leadership, if we look to personality factors alone. In thinking about leadership, we need to ask, "Leadership for what?" Would we want George Patton to direct a hospice, Dick Cheney, the former Vice President who shot his friend in the face having mistaken him for a pheasant, to lead our gun club? Winston Churchill proved a great prime minister for war, but was rejected overwhelmingly once the war was won and peacetime leadership needed. Successful leadership is going to vary according to the task being pursued, the environment surrounding the group, and the nature of the followership available to be mobilized.

Toward the end of a meeting with a board committee of a client company, a business lawyer changes the direction of the discussion. He itemizes the goals implicitly agreed upon and recommends actions to reach them. This is a leaderly act, but he is not the leader of the committee. After his intervention, the chairman of the committee resumes direction of the meeting. The group accepts their attorney's advice and the competent business lawyer resumes his purely consultative role with no need to continue to direct the discussion. To do otherwise, would not be leaderly but inappropriate, even neurotic, an act serving ego rather than task. The lawyer has engaged in an act of leadership, but he is not the leader of the group.

Where there is no great task to grapple with, great leadership cannot occur. It can be argued that Bill Clinton was not a great president, if he could have been, because he was becalmed by peace and prosperity. Confronted with no exigent task, his attention wandered, and he sullied his office.

Where challenging tasks confront the mediocre, disaster looms. Awakened by a great task, George W. Bush finally found his voice. And, as he gained his voice, he lost his way. It turned out that the Iraqis had nothing to do with 9/11, and they had no weapons of mass destruction.

Outside of political settings, leadership is no more a position than it is *primarily* a personality characteristic; it is, mainly, a role requirement that attends to some positions but not all. Even in the military, this variation occurs. A Platoon Leader is just that. General Eisenhower, Supreme Commander of Allied Forces in Europe, was an administrator. He was also a middle son. More about leadership and sibling position later.

Leaderly Managers

Competent management nearly always requires some leadership. Eisenhower had, after all, to order the invasion of Normandy to proceed or not. The first responsibility of managers, as in the Normandy Invasion, at all levels is to regulate exchange across boundaries to insure the viability of their groups. In the law firm, the No. I position, typically that of managing partner, is located on the boundary between the firm as a whole and its environment. *Management of this external boundary—that between firm and environment—is the primary requirement upon this role because enterprise survival depends upon it.*

65

Attempts to foresee the future are required and bets must be made. Connections to important clients, extant and potential, must be made, one or more branch offices need to be opened or closed, mergers or acquisitions attempted, practice area emphases begun or shifted. Proposals must be presented to followers in a manner sufficiently convincing to win support for such measures.

The managing partner who, rather than looking outwards, preoccupies himself primarily with billings and receipts neglects the leadership functions of his position. Only the managing partner has been given the authority to represent the total enterprise, so when he or she fails to lead in relation to the external environment, no one does. Or, worse, several unauthorized and variously motivated individuals lead in different directions. These are usually senior partners who have important clients and are refractory to management control.

It would be far better to have an executive director with a financial background provide the managing partner and executive committee with periodic, accurate, and understandable financial updates, than for a managing partner to preoccupy himself with the green visor work.

Personal Characteristics of Leaders

If we take as defining contexts, the nature of the task being pursued, the enterprise environment, and the available followership, we may yet be able to say something useful about personal characteristics relevant to leadership, for there are some. In the next sections, I will elaborate upon the ones I have found to be important. These derive not from questionnaire studies or laboratory experiments, but from consultation to executives and biographical study of the great. (As one exemplar of the leader, and of instructive history, see Doris Goodwin's biography, *Team of Rivals: The Political Genius of Abraham Lincoln.*)

To mention them briefly, these personal characteristics of leaderly managers are: 1) Embodiment of group aspirations and ideals; 2) long future time-span; 3) enterprise-orientation rather than person-orientation; 4) exercise of authority with minimal self-inflation, hostility or guilt; 5) acceptance of responsibility without perfectionistic self-blame; 6) ability to delegate and supervise generatively; 7) ability to repair injured relationships; and 8) perspective informed by a reading of history and/or a sense of humor.

Where the task centrally involves integration, or the prevention of enterprise fragmentation, a depressive tint to the personality helps, as was the case with Lincoln. Depressive individuals have a particular need to hold things together, lest all hope be lost. In Lincoln's case, he could not bear to see the union dissolve. We think of depression as an illness and seek to drug it away. But a capacity for depression is required for both empathy and creativity. One of Trumps weaknesses as a leader is that he cannot, apparently, be depressed, characterizing himself instead as a "stable genius."

But here again, the particular nature of the task toward whose achievement the leader must lead is determinative. A touch of paranoia may help in mobilizing to attack an external enemy; of mania, where an extraordinary but shorter-term expenditure of energy is needed; narcissism, where identification with a preening leader excites otherwise cynical and dowdy followers; and psychopathy, where the odds are so poor that only unscrupulous trickery can carry the day.

2. Natural and Situational Leadership

Leadership behavior in some people arises from inclinations that are characteristic and longstanding, while in others it is occasioned by particular situations. I call the first type of leader "natural" and the second "situational." One type of leader is not necessarily better than the other. It depends upon the task and the context.

US Presidents provide a good sample for the study of leadership, since we know a lot about them and how they performed. To remove our own amateur sentiments about performance, we can rely upon the rankings of professional historians, as I do below. Agreement among republican and democratic professionals is very high. Further research is needed to add to the observations and discipline the speculations that follow.

Natural Leaders

Followers are able to sense the special disposition of natural leaders. Take, for example, the overwhelming tendency for first-born sons to be both nominated for and elected US President during times of international crisis. Every first born has been the member of a group that was invaded and occupied (i.e., by siblings). Thus, it appears that first-born sons may develop an authoritative protectiveness toward their group—first the family, later the nation. In times of external threat, the electorate responds to this quality. Later-born sons are preferred during times of peace. A similar pattern holds for British Prime Ministers, though less strongly.

There are no only children among American presidents, although three had only half-siblings.

The remarkable thing is that voters and party officials rarely think about the sibling position of a candidate or consider it important. They are reacting to enduring emanations of birth order whose cause escapes them.

Both Obama and his first opponent, McCain, were first-born sons, as was Winston Churchill. Clement Attlee, who unseated Churchill once Germany had been defeated and the peace secured, was a later-born son.

Hillary Clinton is first-born, too. As our sample of female political leaders expands, we will learn whether this matching of sibling order to national task is true for women as well as men. Vice President Kamala Harris, a likely successor to the presidency, is a first born.

It has not been established that natural leaders are usually first-born. Some situational leaders may be offered and accept the reins during times of international conflict. It should also be kept clear that the fact that American and British nominating parties and electorates prefer first-borns during times of international peril does not mean that such leaders actually perform better. We only know that followers tend to believe that they will.

The top five US presidents rated by historians (Washington, Lincoln, Jefferson and the two Roosevelts) were all first born sons. Of the bottom five (Buchanan, Harding, Andrew Johnson, Pierce, and Trump), only two are.

Arguably, of the top five, only FDR can be said to have been elected during a time of international crisis.

Note that the best presidents occur across three centuries, two in the case of the great failures, four of which latter are clustered in the 1800s.

Typically, having had a long resume of elected positions, as natural leaders age they have difficulty giving up control. This is an important and difficult task, one required for good development of both individual and group. As they enter old age, natural leaders need to hand over the reins of power and allow the emergent generation of new leaders behind them to lead. Situational leaders would have less trouble doing so.

When Churchill, the quintessential natural leader and war time prime minister, lost the election at age 70, Clementine, thinking her husband needed a rest, said to him, "This may be a blessing in disguise." Churchill responded, "If so, my dear, the disguise is extraordinarily effective." At 90, his last words to his wife were, "I am so bored."

This generational dynamic was being played out in the 2008 US presidential election. Obama was 47, McCain 72. It is a curious fact that in 2015 those leading in the race for the nomination of their parties were all old—nearly outside of the age distribution that has characterized American presidents throughout our history. Is this a result of the increase in the number of people who survive into old age or the infertility of our political system? The leaders of the two political parties in 2022 are both in their mid-to-late 70s. Are they symbols from the collective unconscious of a way of life coming to an end?

Trump, A Fight Leader

Since the original writing of this book in 2014-15, both of the American septuagenarians were elected president.

Donald Trump was at 70 the oldest person to ever assume the presidency. While, at 77, he was also outside the distribution by age, unlike his predecessor, Biden was qualified by a life time of government experience, including the vice presidency.

Donald Trump was a second born son, ten years younger than his older brother. In 2016, the US faced no unusual foreign menace. It was not a time of national emergency and so, as our studies would have predicted, no first born candidate would have been preferred.

Trump's opponent, Hillary Clinton, was a first born, who nevertheless won the popular vote. After having spent her entire adult life under attack from the right, Hillary's strongest personal valence was, or so it appeared, to fight. It is interesting to consider that among the various reasons adduced for her defeat in the electoral college, her relative unsuitability for leadership as a first born in the absence of war may have played an invisible role. She had been an enthusiastic supporter of the invasion of Iraq a country whose exact geographical location was unclear to her opponent.

A leaders predominant emotional valence strikes a chord or fails to do so in potential followers. These valences are, following the British group theorist Wilfred Bion, *fight-flight*, *pairing*, and *dependency*. Trump, an indulged second born, might have been content simply to be admired. But brought up to believe that the world consisted in winners and losers and that only a weakling might be counted among the latter, his natural inclination when a reversal arose was to protest unfair treatment. Increasingly as his failures in office rose up nearly to cover his head, he issued the lament of the second born son: *"It's not fair!"* To stir his aggrieved but politically inert followers to action, he needed to identify the people who were taking advantage. He chose 'scofflaw' European allies, illegal immigrants, Chinese industrial thieves and virus transmitters, and, ultimately, democrats.

The more militant among his supporters were also weakly educated white men who felt that their uninspiring futures had been unfairly restricted by the preferential treatment of minorities.

When a dependency leader was needed to protect the populace from Covid illness and to inspire trust in his protection, President Trump urged the ingestion of bleach and promised that the virus would go away by itself. Trump lacked a valence for dependency leadership. Taking care of people did not come naturally to him.

The American Political Science Association division on the presidents rated Trump 45th out of 45 in their ratings of best presidents. (Lincoln was first, Obama 8th.) But what would one expect from liberal university professors? The minority subset of republicans rated Trump 40th. One imagines that a ranking based upon the full four year term would have lowered his rating even among the more conservative political scientists

These rating were made after the 'halcyon' days of his first two years, before the full toll of deaths attributable to his negligence had been told and before he had attempted to achieve re-election by *Coup d' Etat*. Prior to the insurrection he inspired after losing re-election, academics argued over whether he fit strict historical criteria to qualify as a fascist. Most thought he did not because of the absence of mobilized political violence and preferred the designation "Authoritarian."

Were there professors in German universities in the early 1930s who were engaged in similar definitional arguments about Hitler even as their offices were being boarded up?

While he has since qualified for the epithet, held up against the pure type of fascist like Hitler and Mussolini, there nonetheless seems to be an important difference. Both Hitler and Mussolini were fight leaders, both were first born sons, and both were serious, if evil, men who wanted to lead. Trump, like Chauncy Gardner in the movie *Being There*, likes to *watch*, as he did, enjoying a Big Mac before the television in the White House for three hours while his supporters invaded the capitol building. Mussolini pursued international status for Italy among the great powers, Hitler a revived economy, territorial expansion and 'racial purity' for Germany. Trump only wanted to be looked at and applauded, before his primary aim was replaced by the desire for revenge.

Some of the conservative ideologues behind Trump were, however, serious all along. As were the certain of the monied interests.

Situational Leaders

Situational leaders come forth to meet a particular task or a particular time, and may not be seen again. These people engage successfully in leadership but are not generally thought of—nor think of themselves— as leaders. Here we have a man or woman, not for all seasons, but for a particular one.

Harry Truman is an example of a successful situational leader. After a series of failures as a small businessman and having shown limited ability as a military and political leader, the role of president was thrust upon him by the death of Roosevelt. When Truman met with the press following the sudden death of FDR and his own swearing in as the 33rd President, he inquired of the assembled reporters if they had ever had a load of hay fall on them. He then asked for their prayers. Yet, Truman was enlarged by the role of the presidency, and he rose to the task. The leadership that Truman displayed by his second term surprised people. He was eligible to run for a third term, but declined.

Historians rate Truman, who was a first born son, among the top ten of the 46 US presidents.

Mixed Types

In many leaders, there is an admixture of the two—a general inclination to lead, with a responsiveness to particular situations. The mixed type is the more usual case in professional service organizations, like law firms, where a managing partner's longstanding motivation has not been to become a general or a president but to develop high-level expertise and success in his or her profession.

Tasks and Contexts

With either type of leadership, quantitative studies of presidential *success* find that circumstantial factors far outweigh personal characteristics. Indeed, not a single pre-presidential personal factor has proved predictive of success in office. As Lincoln wrote, "I claim not to have controlled events, but confess plainly that events have controlled me."

This means that the nature of the task for which leadership is required is generally far more important than the strength of the leadership inclination in the person. Yet in some instances, it may nonetheless be critical. It can be argued that Churchill saved England during the Second World War and that George Washington rescued our nascent republic by leading an army of ill-trained, ill-equipped civilians to victory over a powerful nation's best soldiers. If there was a better man for the former job, no one was recommending him, and if some criticized Winston's strategy, few doubted his leadership. The founders of the US republic urged a victorious Washington to accept the crown as king.

What these findings tell us is not to ignore personal factors but to avoid becoming exclusively preoccupied with them, as we tend so strongly to do.

We cannot know whether McCain would have made a better president than Obama. We are not given a control group in life. The near collapse of the financial markets that occurred just before Obama's election and the deficit caused by years of unfunded wars, could have told the story of his presidency before it began. That it did not, together with Obama's extraordinary achievements in foreign affairs as well as domestic ones, suggests remarkable judgment and strength. It seems likely now that future historians will rate Obama among our few greatest presidents. Writing this now in 2022, we see that scholars have done so (8th to 10th).

Ordinarily, even an outstanding individual trying to exercise leadership cannot do so alone. A leadership coalition is required. As a former community organizer, Obama knew this, but if had a major failing, it was in how long it took him to realize that Republicans would not cooperate with him no matter what he did. His multilateralism found more reasonable partners abroad. And, truth be told, he may have found the European leaders more civilized. Urged to shmoos more with American congressmen, Obama replied, "*You* have a drink with Mitch McConnell!"

Essential Leadership Capacities

In the previous section, I listed eight hallmark capacities of successful leaders. These capacities are ones that I have found in successful executives in a diverse range of enterprises, public and private, large and small, and from the study of biographies of the great. These are all things required of competent leaders whether they lead by habitual inclination or by rising to the requirements of a task.

I shall elaborate on the first of these, *embodiment of group aspirations and ideals*, in section four of this chapter.

Finally, a group makes the best of what leadership resources it has. In some instances, it may have natural leaders who are inappropriate or questionably suitable for the task it confronts. Or, it may have none of these people and must bring forth its best candidate for an exigent situation. In a third case, a group of partners may feel itself to be functioning in a pacific environment and prefer to heave to and drift, allowing a committee of the well-intentioned to administer things. It is important when choosing this last option that partners make certain they are not in the shipping lane, and that the current is not setting them on to a lee shore.

3. Leading Work Group Meetings: The Case of the Resistant Group

It is 8:30 Monday morning and time for the corporate group's departmental meeting. The main agenda item concerns a prospective 'merger.' Of the eighteen attorneys in the group—ten partners and eight associates—six are present in the conference room, including Jeff, the 46-year-old head of the department. He has been a partner for seven years and department head for one. Of the other five people present, two are partners and three are associates. Office premises people are at work setting up juice, coffee, and bagels on the side table.

Attorneys engage in small talk about the local football team's pre-season game. A partner observes that the new coach is extraordinarily determined, if inarticulate. When words fail the coach, his eyes bulge. Another points out that the team president is young and has no management experience. There is agreement that the squad is improving, although some feel that it is still not good enough to compete against teams with deeper benches. An associate points out that there are good players available on the waiver wire. The advantages of strengthening the team versus the risks of introducing new players are weighed.

By 8:40, the remaining five associates have arrived together with two other partners. One of the partners who had been in attendance leaves the room. Eating and small talk continue. The view is expressed that good waiver wire players are usually on the downside of their careers: "If they're so good, why are they being traded?"

It is 8:45 and Jeff doesn't know whether to start the meeting or not. The meeting has no set ending time. The group typically works until it has gotten through the agenda, but only half of the partners are present.

Another partner arrives and puts a bagel in the toaster. An associate leaves the room, and the partner who had left returns. One partner works intently on her iPhone; another talks on his. A paralegal comes into the room to confer with an associate.

The group's most senior partner, Dennis, arrives, pours himself coffee, sits down, and asks a junior partner whether a client he has referred has called. The client is an important Napa Valley vintner who is considering acquiring another winery. He is wealthy and politically connected. The football talk stops and Jeff and the group listen. Dennis says that he can't keep the client himself because of conflicts. It is known that Dennis is under pressure from Alex, the managing partner, to transition his merger & acquisition practice as he nears retirement. Partners doubt that Dennis will do either anytime soon.

Alex had promised growth when he had been elected managing partner two years earlier at 48. Some partners, especially younger ones, were in favor of growth but few partners are in a hurry to do anything about it. Two years into his term, no growth has occurred. New arrivals have been offset by departures. Consultants warn that the legal industry is segmenting and that larger firms are not only the wave of the future but of the present as well. Mid-sized firms, like theirs, are in danger of being swept away. Consultants make a lot of money helping firms merge and urge action. When large firms break apart, the help of consultants is needed then, too.

The failure to make progress has only added to Alex's determination. His preoccupation has earned him the sobriquet, "The Great," among partners. The issue of growth and Alex's leadership of it are not discussed openly in meetings.

At close of business the previous Friday, Alex had invited the members of a tax and estate boutique across town to meet with the corporate group. The night before, on Thursday, he called Jeff at home. He wanted to make certain that the corporate partners talked about the acquisition as a "merger," because the smaller group of tax and estate lawyers liked to think of it that way. Alex instructed Jeff to report back to him on the group's views of the prospective merger immediately after the Monday meeting.

Alex had not involved Jeff in devising his growth strategy. The firm's executive committee, which does not include department heads, has approved the idea, but Jeff isn't sure whether acquiring the tax and estate group is a good move or not. It makes sense to him that the firm needs to grow, but the economy is slow and his group's hours are down. Although, like other department heads, Jeff has not the authority to set compensation—this is done by an elected compensation committee—Alex holds him responsible for the group's productivity. He is expected to goad the attorneys to greater effort, as Dennis had done when he was department head.

Jeff worries about how they will find work for five more partners. The new partners are all reputed to have good books of business, but Dennis has observed that such "books" remind him of what the French say about California wines—they do not travel well. Alex has reassured Jeff that the managing partner of the estate planning boutique has a book of business comparable to Dennis'.

Jeff doubts that Dennis will find this equality welcome. He is concerned about how he will manage a group with two such accomplished senior partners. As it is, a tendency remains for the group to look to Dennis for leadership and for Dennis to take it. If there were rivalry between the two rainmakers, how would he keep it from splitting the group? There was already tension between the tax and the merger & acquisition partners.

It is 8:50 and the remaining members of the group arrive. The associate who had left returned. The paralegal exited. The exchange between Dennis and the junior partner about the referral continues.

Jeff says to the group, "I think we should start."

Group Dynamics

Experienced private practice lawyers will find this problem annoyingly familiar and its solution obvious. Jeff is a weak leader who is intimated by Dennis. He propitiates his senior, because he is afraid that Dennis might get mad and retire precipitously; or, worse, that he will join a competing firm, in either case depriving the corporate group of a significant portion of its revenue. Dennis had been heard threatening to do so more than once. Jeff needs to assert himself and, in effect, call Dennis's bluff; if Dennis doesn't like it, let him leave.

Jeff *is* having trouble leading the group and managing Dennis. But the problem is larger than that. Consider the small talk prior to the formal beginning of the meeting. Such talk often gives metaphorical expression to a group's underlying concerns; in this case, the leadership of the firm and its direction: The leaders are too young, determined but unconvincing, the firm lackluster. They cannot compete with the best teams. Maybe new people should be brought in; maybe bringing in new people would wreck the firm.

View the conversation between Dennis and the junior partner about the referral as enacting the lack of confidence in growth as a business plan: Growth may or may not be good; what counts for sure is well-heeled clients. Dennis has them and from time to time, if he is treated properly, he will pass one down. The group, including Jeff, behaves as if to say, "There is nothing else to talk about."

Departmental Leadership Mirrors Firm Leadership

Jeff's trouble leading the group mirrors the trouble Alex is having leading the firm. Alex wants growth, consultants tell him that the firm needs it, but he has not succeeded in convincing a majority of partners or in creating a leadership coalition of a subset of them. This is especially so with senior partners and there is in this firm the not uncommon struggle between the emerging leadership generation (40-58) and the retiring generation of senior lawyers (58-), a problem upon which we will elaborate in Chapter Seven.

Note, too, that the weakness of the department head is not personal but structural. Jeff has no authority concerning the compensation of the attorneys in his group, and he does not control the assignment of important matters. Alex expects him to get Dennis to transition his practice and mobilize his group in support of firm growth, but since he is not a member of the executive committee, he is not involved in decisions. Jeff is asked to represent a task he has had no hand in crafting, that is not widely embraced, and, without the authority to do so, to command allegiance to shaky leadership.

Withal, regardless of the limits of the authority vested in Jeff's position, he can enrich or impoverish it by his own behavior. He certainly has sufficient authority to lead a needed discussion in the corporate group, analyze it, and report the results.

Managing Group Boundaries

Boundaries, including time boundaries, are essential for competent group functioning and, as previously noted, the leader must use his or her authority to manage them. A leader's failure to do so demoralizes members. Before long, they are likely to become anxious and angry about the absence of leadership and prone to acting out.

This group's boundary is chaotic; people come late, they enter and leave, people who are not members of the group are present. Jeff is not in control of the boundary, yet they are met to consider expanding the boundaries of the group to add new members. In rendering the boundary chaotic, the attorneys are, in effect, resisting Alex's growth agenda. They behave as if to say, "You want to change our group? Don't expect us to help you do it!" Not only do they make it difficult to get a full discussion of adding new members, they make it difficult to even find the group. A group without a boundary is not a group but an aggregate of individuals, in this case solo practitioners. They are like guerillas who blend into the civilian countryside only to reappear and skirmish unpredictably.

In the authority void created by Jeff's inaction, Dennis dominates the group and acts out, with group support, an unresolved issue of leadership succession. Dennis knows that Jeff is having trouble establishing his authority and that members continue to look to him for leadership. Knowing this, it would be better if he avoided undermining Jeff. More sophisticated followership on Dennis's part would be to inquire into the referral matter briefly and quietly, suggest that they talk about it later, then look to Jeff to begin the meeting. In the history of American law firms, there are at least two accounts of the occurrence of this level of sophisticated cooperation from senior partners. Both may be apocryphal.

Strengthening The Time Boundary

What sense would it make to start the meeting on time without a quorum? First, the department is not part of a political entity but of a commercial one, so the idea of quorums is, in that sense, inappropriate. Further, time is a limited resource in every human enterprise, none more so than one in which professionals are selling it at high rates to meet hefty billable hour requirements.

By 8:40, half of the partners and a majority of the group are present. Jeff can wait until then to start if he wants, but he should tell the group that he is doing so. In this way, he keeps control of the group by using his authority explicitly to delay the beginning of the meeting rather than passively acquiescing to the delinquency of the missing attorneys. Also by noting that the time boundary is not being observed, he reminds the group that it exists.

Like many management acts, this one needs to be done consistently and persistently until a norm of reasonable punctuality has been established. Naturally suspicious partners can be expected to find it worrying to join a departmental meeting that is already in progress. If, nonetheless, a significant portion of the group continues to be delinquent, this problem should be placed on the agenda for discussion: Why won't people come on time? Do they arrive late because they doubt that any real work can get done in the group? Have they interpreted Jeff's laissez-faire approach to starting meetings to mean that he agrees? Do they view the request for their views on merger and other firm issues as a sham, because Alex and the executive committee will try to do what they want and can't do much anyway?

Work group leaders often fear to broach such subjects lest open discussion make things worse. It may temporarily. Yet experience teaches that if such problems are systemic, they rarely go away by themselves. Left unspoken, they lead more often to sudden, surprising departures of attorneys. Leaders should look for help from consultants who are trained and experienced in directing discussions of group process.

Starting The Meeting

It goes without saying that Jeff should be seated at the head of the table. In a group with such poorly established leadership, sitting anywhere else would symbolize an abdication of authority and compound the problem of starting late. Were his leadership better established, it would not matter much where he sat. When he does begin the meeting, Jeff should start with a statement of the task. This should be combined with a comment about the time boundary problem: "I'm concerned about the late start that we're getting, because we have an important question to consider. What do we think of the tax and estate people we met Friday? Do we want them to join our group? Alex has asked me to report our views to him after the meeting. Who would like to begin?" Note that Jeff expresses the concern about lateness in terms of the task not in terms of his personal feelings.

We know who would begin. It will be Jeff's responsibility to ensure that Dennis does not dominate the discussion and that all views get aired. Group members permitted to remain silent are often holding valuable ideas and are apt to sabotage group decisions outside of the meeting.

A group with a well-managed time boundary has a set ending time. In this example, let's say it is 9:30. The meeting begins at 8:30 and ends at 9:30, give or take a few minutes at either point. What's the matter with continuing until the work is done? The discussion will wander and the group will suffer from the removal of a bracing piece of reality: *time is passing, their competitors are working, and they are mortal.* Groups need all the help they can get to avoid becoming unrealistic and in other ways incompetent, and only good leadership and effective structure, like well-managed boundaries, keep their collective heads above water. If an hour is insufficient for the task of a particular meeting, a competent leader anticipates this and creates a special meeting of longer duration—again with set time boundaries. If a meeting lasts more than an hour and a half, regression in mental functioning is predictable.

A well-led meeting does not run out of time. The leader monitors it throughout and keeps the group apprised. "We only have another twenty-five minutes. We are in general agreement about a, let's move on to b." If a matter cannot be resolved or moved ahead sufficiently in the time allotted, an extra meeting can be set—again with established time boundaries. E.g., "Let's meet again for an hour tomorrow morning at 8:30."

4. Psychodynamics of Leader-Follower Relations I

It is January 2008 and you are sitting in your living room with a friend watching Hillary and Barack debate. You and your friend are well educated and politically knowledgeable. To you, Hillary comes off as calculated, clever, and cliché-ridden, while Barack seems genuine, thoughtful and articulate. Your friend thinks that Hillary is smart, courageous, and determined and finds Barack pedantic, vague, and soft. Not only do you and your friend have divergent impressions, you are both convinced of their validity. Argument is useless.

How can this be? You are looking at exactly the same data and you are both justified in regarding yourselves as objective, rational people. Objective, rational people can disagree about issues, but we are not talking about issues, but rather perceptions of a leader's character.

In earlier sections of this chapter, I enumerated eight personal characteristics relevant to leadership and promised to elaborate on at least the first of these, the embodiment of group aspirations and ideals.

Personifying Group Ideals

This first characteristic is at issue in the above vignette. How does a leader come to be seen as personifying a group's aspirations and ideals? First, it helps if this is substantially true. For example, it appears unarguably to be the case that Barack is thoughtful and Hillary determined. If thoughtfulness is high among a group's ideals, the group takes that aspect of Barack's personality and wraps it around the entirety. A group of Clinton supporters may do the same thing with determination in assessing her personality.

Transference Projections Towards Leaders

In reality, both personalities are multi-faceted. Even a moment's dispassionate thought is sufficient to remind us that Barack, too, is highly determined and Hillary is very thoughtful. To make thoughtfulness Barack's distinguishing characteristic and determination Hillary's requires psychological work on the part of followers. They do this work with unconscious projections; followers transfer feelings about important adults from childhood to the adult leaders of today. This *transference* operates without the knowledge of the transferer and transference is always, in some degree, ambivalent.

One of Freud's earliest discoveries was that this happens in psychotherapy and that without a positive transference from patient to therapist, little can be accomplished. While he found transference to be an aid, he also learned that it could sink the ship; the ambivalent nature of the transference, he came to warn, meant that it had to be handled like an unstable chemical.

In psychotherapy, there is nowhere else for the negative, hostile part of the transference to go other than towards the doctor; unless, abetted by a poorly trained psychotherapist, the patient acts out the negative transference outside the consulting room toward parents, siblings, employers, spouses, partners and the like. These sorts of acting out produce drama and crises, which the all-good therapist can use to advise the patient on how better to deal with the inadequate and ill-motivated people who surround him. This sort of collusion, usually unwitting, is common.

Splitting of Ambivalence Towards Leaders

In American political life, the two party system lends itself to splitting of the transference. In idealizing a leader—making the part of his or her personality we value most its entirety—the negative part of our ambivalence is split off and projected into his or her opponent. In this manner, our attachment to the leaders we like is intensified and their superiority to those we do not like is enhanced not only by the aforementioned projection but also by *splitting*.

Regression

As unconscious mental mechanisms, splitting and projection are well known to psychotherapists who treat the mentally ill. They are characteristic psychological mechanisms in borderline and schizophrenic patients. They are also typical of very young children. Transference relations of followers to leaders can stimulate *regression* to such primitive states of mind.

Henry Adams famously said, "Politics have always been the systematic organization of hatreds." Where else do otherwise rational adults allow themselves such extremes of passionate partiality, where opinion becomes knowledge and sentiment a guide? Where else but in our relations with leaders—and in romance and war—do we react so childishly?

Emotional Feedback Loops Between Leaders and Followers

Emotions between followers and leaders do not run one way only. What followers project, leaders *internalize*. And, processes of *internalization* are as unconscious and irrational as are those of projection and splitting. Anyone who has taught seminars or worked with juries has experienced this. One group makes you smart, another one makes you stupid. In one group, your jokes are funny, in another insulting. In front of the first group, one's knowledge, memory and imagination are enhanced. For reasons that often precede you and arise from their feelings about each other or the leadership of the organization that has required them to attend, this group has adopted a positive transference towards you. In a meeting with a different, dyspeptic group, you find your IQ drops, memory shorts, and imagination dries up.

A Personal Example

In the dawn of the 2001 recession, I did a workshop on mentoring for the branch office of a Silicon Valley law firm. The presentation was enthusiastically received. We hit it off right away. Before long, I abandoned my power point and spoke extemporaneously. The partners listened to my ideas, gave serious attention to my recommendations, and laughed, weeping at my jokes.

They especially liked this one: "Associates who enjoy authentic mentor relationships are unlikely to leave the firm. So, in providing them with mentors, don't think of it as kindness. Think of it as revenge. They will end up living the same exhausting lives that you are living!"

Afterwards, a senior litigator came up to me and said that I had the talent of the best courtroom lawyers, that he had listened to every word I had said and I had not missed a beat.

One week later, I made the same presentation to the main office. I began as before with my power point slides. Very quickly attorneys interrupted with hostile questions and objected to my efforts to amuse them. The head of the mentoring committee, his back turned to me, shouted to his partners," Our lives are not awful!" At the first break, the partner who was responsible for continuing legal education workshops told me I was losing my audience. He was right. I felt like I was swimming in mud.

I hadn't changed and neither had the material. It was the different states of mind—*transference dispositions*, I believe—of the two groups that were determinative. The first group was disposed to like me, the second not to. In the first group, there quickly occurred *a positive projection-positive internalization feedback loop* that made them happy and brought out the best in me; in the second, *a negative projection-negative internalization feedback loop* was quickly formed that made them angry and brought out the worst in me as a presenter. I do not know the origins of these dispositions, but I have a clue and a speculation.

In the main office, the room in which I was to make my presentation had chairs neatly arranged for the audience and a space of empty floor in front for the speaker—no podium, no table, no chair, nothing. It was as though leadership had disappeared and had left behind no provision for others to lead.

Indeed, during those days, the managing partner of the firm, an attorney from the home office, was frequently absent. It was rumored he was meeting with representatives of large Eastern firms to talk about mergers. The managing partner had endorsed the mentoring initiative. What authority I had to lead the meeting came from him, yet he had stuck us in a room together without even a by your leave to his partners or to me.

Were the home office partners mad at him for being an absent leader about to sell them to the highest bidder in whose large firm they, too, would become merely a branch office? Were they scapegoating me for his neglect and 'disloyalty'? If so, why hadn't the partners in the branch office reacted that way? Perhaps they had long felt marginal, and, as the storm clouds of the recession gathered on the horizon, perhaps they had developed a manic desert island mentality, gaily enjoying their last bottle of wine and happy to have such good entertainment at the end. Was there also a manic anticipation of revenge at the likelihood that soon they would all be branch offices and their managing partner just another partner, living the same "awful" lives as the rest of them? It really had seemed to be my use of the word "revenge" in the associate mentoring joke that had brought the house down.

If correct, how does one apply insights such as these? Here is one application. Projections from followers can make a leader feel *constrained* from acting, as though assailed by the accusations of persecuted children; or, alternately, *impelled* to act, as though moved by the cries for help of needy, deserving ones. Internalizing such emotion-laden projections can erode a leader's judgment and result in bad mistakes.

Leaders need access to their own inner lives—wishes, fears, dreams, moods—in order to weigh them accurately. Extremes of paralysis and impulsion are a tip off. Leaders who tend generally to swing back and forth, will find it more difficult to know when followers are manipulating their emotions. The more even-tempered will find it easier to identify the projections. Obama would appear to be an example of the latter.

In my case, I acknowledged to the group the difficulty we were having, expressed regret, and then, perhaps satisfied to see that I was suffering too, the partners allowed me to soldier on unmolested for the remainder of my presentation.

5. Psychodynamics of Leader-Follower Relations II

Great creative achievements are typically accomplished by individuals working alone. As examples among many, we think of Michelangelo's Sistine Chapel, Gauguin's Tahitian paintings done in self-imposed exile, the carefully woven protective cocoon of Freud's professional isolation as he wrote the *Interpretation of Dreams*, and Einstein's "thought experiments" from which grew his theories of relativity.

Lawyers, professors, engineers—the primary workers in professional service organizations—are highly trained individuals who also have strong needs for autonomy. These professionals may feel that real work goes on best when they work alone. They are more or less content to have people like themselves in other offices, too, but rarely see any compelling reason to collaborate with them. For such men and women, the presence of managers seems even more gratuitous. What are they for? Most come to accept the existence of managers as inessential nuisances, in the same spirit that they accept tendonitis and tooth decay.

Whereas works of innovation and creativity are often best conceived alone, the execution of some tasks, such as large matter litigation or corporate work, requires more than one person and with tasks such as these leadership is needed to organize effort. Where natural leaders are present, they step forward or are chosen. Where there are none, a person unaccustomed to lead but with a keen sense of the special requirements of the task, or the exigencies of the situation, takes the role. While managing a department or even an entire business may seem mundane, it is nonetheless true that an element of leadership is involved in getting workers to accept group goals. To go beyond acceptance and secure their best efforts, leaders will need to inspire workers.

Envy Toward Leaders

We want our leaders to be better than us, but perhaps not too much better. Great leaders can evoke painful envy. If, to use a current example, the leader studied international relations at Columbia University, our own degree in sports broadcasting from Bucolic U may seem unimportant. If our president can make a three point jump shot in basketball, we may be made nostalgic for youthful arches that have long since fallen. If his spouse is tall and smart and beautiful, our own may seem dowdy and short. If his children appear to love and admire him, we are reminded that ours tend to avoid us. If his decisions avert an international financial crisis, we feel grumpy and dyspeptic about the deficit. Should he win the Nobel Prize, an inclination to share in the collective pride may be quickly soured by the question: "When will I get the recognition *I* deserve?"

Ambivalence Toward Leaders

Our admiration for a leader, as with other emotional attachments, may be infiltrated with envy. The same emotional forces that lead to idealization can quickly lead to hostility. This is especially true of dependency relationships, such as that which typically exists between follower and leader. The experience or perception of unmet dependency needs arouses a special fury. As noted, this was one of Freud's first discoveries in treating neurotic patients: the patient's transference on to the doctor of gratitude originally felt toward parents could easily become hostile, for the doctor must inevitably frustrate as did the parents.

Ambivalence is uncomfortable and poses a challenge to our belief in ourselves as rational, consistent people. Unconscious defensive maneuvers arise to dispense with it. We have described splitting earlier, a mechanism by which the positive and negative aspects of the emotion are separated and the pure distillates invested in different persons or groups; e.g., "democrats are good, republicans are bad," when in reality, the performance of both parties is nothing to write home about. Or, "the Oakland (sic) Raiders are on the way down; the San Francisco 49ers have a fine coach," when on any given Sunday, the teams are scarcely distinguishable.

Identifying with Leaders

In accepting leadership, individual workers become followers. They accept that higher status and greater reward are bestowed on one person or subset of persons. When this is done enthusiastically, it is because followers invest a quantum of their self-love in the leader, seeing him or her as the embodiment of their ideals. Why is it self-love that is given? Because it is the only kind of love we have. But narcissism, too, is limited, and its expenditure is felt.

Identification Across Group Boundaries

Identification helps to make up the narcissistic deficit. The identification also serves to stabilize the ambivalence in a positive direction. Followers feel enhanced, made more than they are, by identifying with a leader who is bigger, smarter, more accomplished, better looking, braver, luckier, or richer, and as members of his or her group, followers feel that they are better than members of other groups. Such as this occurs between the unwashed among Trumps followers and the sparkling billionaire. In an exchange of narcissistic projections, the leader may also come to idealize the group. This may be what is going on when we hear politicians referring to "the American People," as though it were a lustrous, deserving group, rather than an aggregate of the dimwitted, the selfish, and the vengeful.

Identification occurs most naturally with leaders who are members of our own primary groups. It is complicated by differences in age, race, gender and the like. Women workers in male dominated professions have long experienced this obstacle to their own development, as have minority members. Cross-gender identifications seem especially difficult, even as we are learning more about the obstacles to cross-racial identification. For some white people, Obama's success diminishes them.

Here is an example. A former head of a litigation department refused to help its new, female leader with a difficult group problem, even though he had stepped down voluntarily and the help needed was help he could easily provide. "Why should I?" he asked. I replied, "Because you are the former leader of the group, and you want it to prosper." This otherwise kind, fair-minded and accomplished man was completely unmoved by my encouragement. It seemed clear that he felt no emotional connection with the new leader, whatsoever. For him, identifying with her was out of the question. And, if the group were going to embrace her leadership, he would no longer care about it, either. He would withdraw his love and reinvest it fully in himself, restored as the sovereign monarch of a group of one. Men who are out of touch with or frightened by their own femininity resist identifying with female leaders.

Scrutiny of Leaders

Research has shown that extra scrutiny tends to be given to leaders who are women and minorities. It is as though critics find their being in positions of leadership so violative of the natural order of things that it requires exacting examination.

Careful scrutiny always reveals errors. Leadership is a messy, imprecise business and cannot be done perfectly. Under the pressure of magnified scrutiny amid negative expectations, a woman or minority leader needs a strong ego with very good boundaries to keep from being drawn into a defensive and futile attempt at perfection. There is also the danger of being provoked into a loss of self-control that proves the majoritarian theory of the leader's inadequacy correct. When he or she succeeds in maintaining self-control and good boundaries, the leader must then be prepared to be attacked as passive and indifferent or "professorial."

Thus, the expectable burdens of leadership are compounded for women and minorities by the necessity of fending off negative stereotypes and, for the truly exceptional, erosive envy. The same group dynamics surround majority leaders, too, but ordinarily with lesser virulence. President Nixon cursed the Kennedy's as "pretty boys."

6. Following Leaders

Perhaps because we miss the fathers of our childhoods—the fathers we had, or imagined we had, or wished we had had—a mystique bordering on longing surrounds the subject of leadership. At a symposium of business consultants, an otherwise thoughtful organizational psychologist exclaimed that he had "a passion for leadership!" Really? Had he forgotten that Hitler and Mussolini were, for a time, effective leaders as were Stalin and Mao, not to mention Jim Jones?

Despite these and a host of other famous examples of destructive leaders, the glorification continues unabated. Meanwhile, we speak of followers as if only a passive, subservient person would willingly accept such a role. Jack Welch, former Chair and CEO of General Electric, liked to say that if you are not the lead dog, the view never changes. In Welch's canine homily, leadership is not only exalted, followership is reduced to a disgusting abasement. Welch did not mention that if there is only a lead dog, the sled won't move, or that the differences between enterprises led and staffed by people and sleds pulled by dogs are so great as to make the analogy useless. Mr. Welch also failed to tell us how a leader with this conception of followers gains their support. Was he imagining that everyone who cooperates with leaders is content to be considered anally fixated?

Who, it might be asked instead, but a person with a mood disorder and a pathological need to dominate others would want to lead every group he or she is in?

Competent Followership

Aided however uncertainly by a substantial literature on the attributes and practices of great leaders, there is little help to be found on being a good follower or on competent followership. If we can get past the embarrassment at even being interested in such a problem, it may prove instructive to look into the matter.

A competent follower is someone who understands the task being pursued, values it, has requisite skills to do his part, and predicates his behavior on helping to achieve the goal. Influencing and supporting responsible leadership is part of the follower's competence. Some people know intuitively how to do this. Others need directives. Below, I offer some based upon my experience consulting with work groups and their leaders, leading groups myself, and attempting, quite imperfectly, to be a good follower in others. Followers can use the list to measure and sharpen their skills. Leaders can use it to evaluate the kind of support they are getting.

Practices For Competent Followers

1. Attend meetings scrupulously. Take group participation as a serious matter that requires the same high level of responsibility given to other aspects of your work. Particularly in groups under 12, which is the size of most work groups, the absence of a member hurts a group's morale by suggesting, at least in effect, that the work of the group is unimportant. Absences also disrupt continuity and tend to slow momentum. If you can't be at a meeting, transmit your thoughts on the agenda to the leader in advance. If the leader does not prepare and circulate agendas, help the leader to understand the importance of doing so. Knowing your absence in advance, the leader can mention it and avoid the perception of haplessness.

2. Arrive on time and prepared to advance or improve the agenda. This requires thought beforehand. Some people show up at meetings in the same vacant, spectatorial and delinquent state of mind of students attending a high school assembly. Do not be one of them.

3. As you sit in a meeting, ask yourself what contribution you can make, including being silent, that will best move the group forward in pursuit of its task. I call this *sophisticated role behavior,* and it is the mark of a mature, disciplined worker. Naïve role behavior consists in contributing simply because you feel impelled to, or failing to contribute because you feel disinclined.

Eschew the illusion that the meeting is a suitable stage for displays of cleverness and other charming personal qualities or one suitable for catharsis of anger and pique. If you need catharsis, go into psychotherapy.

Avoid confronting the leader in public. An individual leading a meeting is in a very vulnerable position. He or she is outnumbered and exposed to confusing crosscurrents of group sentiment and argument. A leader's capacity to use aggressive criticism in this situation is very limited, although timely, dispassionate, task-oriented rather than personal correction may be usable. A constructive follower will consider saving the corrective conversation for a private discussion.

Ask yourself what pairings, including rivalries with other followers, you are engaged in, within the meeting and without, that subdivide the group and undermine the leader or make his or her work more difficult.

It is a curious phenomenon that members who smirk, gesture, joke and whisper with others in the group believe themselves to be invisible. In reality, this sort of childish behavior is obvious and highly distracting to the person leading the meeting and trying to get work done. It is one example of the kind of regression that individuals in groups undergo if their adult sense of task dedication lags, and if the groups are not well led.

A lack of clarity about the meeting's task or its importance may be the culprit in promoting this sort of regression. So may a lack of clear time boundaries for the meeting. It is the responsibility of leadership to define tasks and establish boundaries. Should the leader fail to do so, a member can help by asking at the beginning of the meeting for a clarification of its purpose and its ending time. If the response is, "to touch base," or "we will take as long as necessary to finish the work," a member should be apprised that the leader does not understand the importance of task clarity or its dependence on well-managed boundaries. Such a leader stands in need of a private, educative conference with a more sophisticated member or a coach.

6. Develop empathy for the leader. Realize that the pressure on the leader's role far exceeds that on your own. Understand that while you must only meet the requirements of your own role, the leader is responsible for everything that happens in his or her group.

Consistent practice of these suggestions by followers will strengthen leaders and enhance overall task performance. But it may seem that I am asking creative people to behave as though they were without personality. Where is the fun? The fun resides in the satisfaction of being a contributing member of a group that realizes a worthwhile goal.

Of course, some leaders do not deserve support. The ends they pursue are destructive or their methods corrupt. When leaderly irresponsibility reaches intolerable levels, a subordinate must consider ways to remove him or resign.

Most leaders fall in the middle range. They are not very good at leading, but they try hard and are genuinely concerned about their members and the enterprise as a whole. Keep in mind that you would have trouble performing their roles, too, and that the causes of their incompetence often originate at organizational levels above them. For example, even where the leader is CEO, his or her work may be seriously compromised by a board chair.

While you anguish and wax eloquent to colleagues about the incompetence of your leader, suspect that the disappointment of your need to have admirable leaders is balanced by the gratification of your wish to see them fail. It is the latter that a competent follower learns to subordinate in the service of task performance.

Chapter Four
Managing the Group

1. Managing the Work Group

Work groups are a common feature of modern organizational life. There are boards of directors, executive committees, departmental and staff meetings and *ad hoc* committees of various kinds. Ordinarily the work group is created to carry out a specific task and the task is suggested by the group's title: e.g., the advisory committee, executive committee or budget committee.

The work group provides an important link between the organization and the individual. From the point of view of the organization, the group serves as a mechanism to accomplish or to undermine diverse organizational goals. From the point of view of the individual, the work group offers an opportunity to learn about the organization and have a voice in the shaping of its goals and practices—or in which he can experience the group's incompetence and lack of authority and his own powerlessness within it.

By and large, work groups do not work very well. They do little either to accomplish organizational tasks or to elicit the responsible, constructive participation of individual members. The resultant costs to both the organization and the individual members are high. Certain organizational goals can only be pursued collectively. In the law firm, work group failure reduces the strength of the firm to that of an aggregate of solo practitioners. For the individual, the failure promotes cynicism about the firm and reinforces a self-protective isolation.

The Primary Task

The management of effective work groups requires informed thought. Putting eight bright and well-intentioned people in a room with an ambiguously defined task won't succeed. To be effective, a group needs good leadership, appropriate structure, and the right composition. The particular leadership, structure and composition should be derived from the nature of the group's *primary task*. There is no other rational basis upon which to make these choices.

What does "primary task" mean? Task is used here in the sense of goal. For the enterprise as a whole, the primary task is that task which must be achieved for the system to survive. In the law firm, the primary task is the generation of profit through the sale of legal services. As other examples, in the university, it is the education of students, in the hospital, the cure of patients. For a constituent group within the organization, its particular primary task is that group's *raison d'être* and will be connected more or less clearly to one or another of the firm's major tasks.

Multiple Major Tasks

Organizations often and groups sometimes have multiple major tasks. A board of directors, for example, typically has the major tasks of policy determination and oversight, where oversight focuses especially upon finances and the evaluation of the CEO. An example of policy determination in a California law firm would be the board's setting of the goal of becoming a transpacific firm, establishing offices throughout Asian Pacific countries. The operations required to do so would be the responsibility of firm management. The board's oversight function would involve monitoring the managing partner's efforts to achieve this goal and the effects on costs and revenue.

In firms that are moving ahead rather than drifting hove to, the direction setting policy task should be primary. In a firm in which the maintenance of revenue and the control of costs are paramount, the oversight task takes precedence. Thus, whether the policy determination task or the oversight task ought to be primary depends upon the current state of the firm and its hopes for the future.

A group can have multiple major tasks, but it cannot have multiple *primary* tasks. It is the responsibility of leadership to determine the relative priority among a group's tasks (primary, secondary, tertiary) and to see that resources—including time and energy—are allocated accordingly. In professional service organizations, the primary institutional resource is people. Leadership must concern itself with the size and composition of the group and insure that the right people are in the group and the wrong people not.

Here Size is Important

Group size matters. Work groups rarely exceed 15 or 16 in number and are usually smaller. Eight to twelve is typical. As size increases beyond 15 or so, the tasks the group is capable of performing become simpler. These larger groups may, for example, meet for the exchange of information or the ratification of proposals created in smaller groups. Even at 12, a group will usually have one or two members who rarely speak. As size diminishes to eight and below relations may become more intimate and complex decision-making possible. A stable set of relationships can evolve. Communication improves as individuals come to understand each other and trust is possible. Below six, family dynamics rear their goofy head, including sibling rivalry. At two, a grouplet is in danger of becoming isolated and perilously divorced from reality, besotted with the kind of lunacy to which pairs are famously prone.

Task Displacement

Too often in groups, tasks are confused with methods. Asked what the task of a recruitment committee is, a member may reply, "to review vita." Actually, the reviewing of documents is merely one of a number of possible ways of performing the task of recruiting talented associates. It is important to keep the distinction between methods and goals clear, lest the methods get sanctified and the illusion develop that the group is succeeding when it is doing things 'the right way.' For example, giving exacting review to the vita of associates year after year, even as the number of accepted offers declines.

As noted earlier, I call the unwitting elevation of methods to the status of goals "task displacement." Groups that are overly concerned with methods become conformist, overly critical of deviance, and prone to scapegoating.

Priority and Compatibility Among Major Tasks

Groups rarely have more than three major tasks. For example, a teaching hospital has the tasks of patient care, training of medical professionals, and research, with patient care being primary. Where there appear to be more, it usually means that components of a complex task are being enumerated separately or that a support function, such as recruitment, is being unwittingly elevated to the status of a major task.

Why does this matter? As noted, identification of the primary task and clarity about the priority among major tasks provides a rational basis for decisions about the allocation of resources and the requisite leadership, structure and composition of the enterprise as a whole and of its constituent groups. Such clarity also allows us to see the degree of compatibility among the major tasks and to take steps proactively to prevent the interference of work on the primary task by work on a secondary one. It also allows us to see when a secondary major task is being excessively subordinated to the primary one. Where task priorities are unclear and tasks imperfectly compatible, work on one task will act as a constraint upon the performance of another.

To return to the teaching hospital as an example, the excessive recruitment of PhD/M.D. physician researchers, will compromise the treatment of patients. Unchecked, it may also lead to a cultural atmosphere in which patients are implicitly seen and dealt with as research subjects. In the law firm, the recruitment committee, in which inadvertently most members are litigators, leads to an overemphasis upon law schools strong in litigation in a firm trying to develop patent and trademark law practices in Asia.

Most importantly, clarity about primary task provides a rational basis for the assessment of organizational effectiveness.

Managers who create and staff work groups need to avoid "good values rationalizations." Ideas of representativeness, constituencies, and fairness need to be subordinated to concerns about competence and productivity. As indicated earlier, professional service organizations are commercial enterprises not political entities and democratic procedures may not always be appropriate. The people who ought to be in the work group are those who have the willingness and expertise to contribute to the achievement of its primary task. Those who should not be in the group are those who are too valuable at what they are doing to be taken off of it, or who would only duplicate the competence of others, or who have no special interest or knowledge relevant to the group's task. Making decisions of this kind is a leaderly act and defending them, another burden of management.

2. Management Principles: The Case of Jaundice, Rancor, and Bile, LLP

Jaundice, Rancor, and Bile, LLP is based in Seattle with several offices throughout the Pacific Northwest, including one in Spokane. An executive committee headed by George, who is the managing partner, runs JR& B. There are also five practice group leaders. Riley is head of the litigation practice group and is in the Spokane office.

Uriah, a litigation partner in Spokane, is thought to be engaged in shady dealings and is chewing up associates. As concern intensifies in Spokane, Uriah asks Riley to transfer him to Seattle. Riley does so. Some time later, George discovers that Uriah is in the Seattle office. "How," George fumes, "could that passive-aggressive S.O.B., Riley, transfer Uriah over here without talking to me about it?"

The answer is that the structure provides for it. Riley has the right to authorize the transfer because he is litigation practice leader. He does not have to consult George, since, in common with the other practice group leaders, he has no reporting relationship to him. In a small firm, the practice group leaders might form the executive committee. In a large firm, they might constitute an operations committee chaired by the managing partner who would report to the chairman of a strategy and policy board, elected by the equity partners.

Instead, JR&B's organizational structure makes no connection between practice group leaders and upper management. Speaking anatomically, the firm's brain and skeletomuscular system are disconnected.

Where an integrating link should exist between practice group and top management there is instead empty space. Riley's passive aggressiveness may have predisposed him to exploit and enjoy the opportunity to dump Uriah on Seattle, but it did not create it. Every human being has some inclination to act in anti-social ways; good structure discourages these negative inclinations and encourages the collaborative, responsible sides of our natures.

Structure requires leadership. The primary responsibility for the unexpected heaping of Uriah on Seattle rests not with Riley but with top management. It is their job to create and manage a structure that integrates the overall enterprise. If we are going to call Riley passive aggressive, we shall have to call top management irresponsible, although in fact they are mainly just unknowing and overworked.

The above example invites incredulity. Yet, it did occur in a well-known, highly regarded law firm. In fact, while it is now common for US firms to be divided into practice groups, their membership—even their existence—is often a matter of interpretation and the place of the practice group leader in the management structure obscure. Were they not routinely ignored, laundry lists of "To dos For Practice Group Leaders" provided by consultants with little understanding of organizational structure would only add to the disorganization.

Practical Theory and Action

For the busy manager, considerations of organizational structure seem too abstract. What's wanted is advice on what to do, and in the next section of this chapter I will offer ten specific recommendations. Yet good theory helps. For example, the notion of culture is commonplace in the law firm. But, as the anthropologists tell us, there can be no culture without social structure and the two are always intertwined. A firm's cultural values will be institutionalized to some degree in its structure. In the current example, the high value on the professional autonomy of the individual lawyer in JR&B's culture is actualized in a loose management structure. Attempts to change the culture of the firm to make it more business-like will require a change in its structure.

Any task will occasion structural arrangements as patterns develop and habits form about who engages in which part of the work, and who decides what. Once in place, structural arrangements help to determine productivity as well as satisfaction and stress. Bad structure fetters and obstructs the competent worker and, in time, dispirits him. Facilitative structure releases productive energy and frees the person to work. Facilitative or obstructive, structure is resistant to change. Leaders need to choose these arrangements deliberately and, once chosen, monitor them and make ongoing the modifications required by changes in the firm's internal state and marketplace.

Facilitating Structure

A facilitating structure not only frees the individual worker to exercise his or her competence, it will take care of various problems with minimal managerial foresight. Had JR&B had an executive or operations committee that included all of the practice group leaders and run by George, he would not have been surprised by bad apples rolling in from Eastern Washington. He would have known about the Uriah problem and been deliberating upon its solution, since it would have been Riley's routine obligation to report it to him and the other practice group leaders in the regular meetings of the operations committee.

Had Riley failed to do so, this would have constituted a serious breach of responsibility and warranted a critical examination of his ability and motives.

Good structure can also mitigate the effects of lackluster leadership, as the history of the American presidency clearly shows. Without a facilitating structure, the enterprise must rely upon brilliance, requiring omniscient, heroic, energetic and lucky leaders. There are not many of these.

How does one go about creating a facilitating structure? There is no single best structure: managers must consider firm goals and the marketplace in which these are being pursued, as well as the resources, human and otherwise, available for work. Within moral and legal limits, a facilitating structure is that which best enables people to achieve the firm's primary task and enjoy the good morale that comes with competent participation.

Primary Task

A Booz Allen Hamilton study showed that nearly 90% of shareholder value lost in the dot com recession of 2001 resulted from inadequate managerial foresight and supervision. A manager must know which among the firm's various tasks is primary. The structure erected to achieve it should consist of a division of labor into specific roles and a division of authority into strata that establishes a hierarchy of accountability among them.

In law firms, this pertains primarily to the management structure, since for most attorneys role differentiation is minimal. Each attorney occupies the same role as many others; i.e., associate, partner, senior partner, or of counsel.

Among the subset of partners who are in management, supervision and coaching help individuals establish priority among the requirements of their roles and learn how best to balance and meet them. Managing role relations with others where productive interdependence is needed can be especially challenging. As managers, attorneys have *de facto* embarked upon a second career for which law school and legal work have neither disqualified nor prepared them.

3. Management Principles: Ten Suggestions

Americans tend to be impatient with complexity and suspicious of prolonged thought. We love "keys" to success and brief lists of "do's and don'ts" that promise to help us lose weight and amass wealth.

Behavioral pre- and proscriptions for managers appear frequently, a recent one being Jack Welch's "Eight Rules" for leaders. Most are empirically derived and their recommendations are unconnected one to the other by any theory or formal conception of the organization. Each is useful to the extent that it illuminates, however briefly.

I offer below my ten suggestions for effective management. Freud wrote that if analysts religiously followed his advice regarding psychoanalytic technique they would soon find themselves in great difficulty. In psychoanalysis, Freud argued, there was no substitute for intuition and in management there is none for "feel," a point made by Mr. Welch himself.

My recommendations are based upon a theory of organizational structure arising from many years of research and consulting and the direct experience of management as clinic director, faculty chairman, and graduate school dean. Each suggestion aims at strengthening the structure of the enterprise so that managers are freed to imagine, think, and plan.

Suggestions

1. Manage structure not just people. Structure comes first. Cold as it sounds, the structure is more important for task performance than the people who fill its roles, because a bad structure will defeat competent individuals and a good one will generate overachievement. Bad structure also creates stress, lowering productivity, reducing retention, and damaging marriages, families, and health.

I consulted with a law firm that had no executive director to head administration. I asked why and was told that they had once had one, but that she was so annoying about accounts receivables that she was let go and the firm resolved never to have one again. It was as though a football team had no equipment manager and when asked about it said that they used to have one but she had been such a nag that they concluded that it would be better to abolish the position and have each player clean and repair his own equipment.

In a rational system, positions exist to perform functions necessary to the achievement of tasks. An important requirement on the role of manager is to create, staff and monitor a structure that enables productive work. If a necessary function is being performed poorly, you get rid of the incumbent not the position. Better yet, supervise the person in a generative manner, and if that doesn't work hire a coach.

Keep the structure as clear and simple as possible. Cooperatively inclined workers need to know where their roles exist in relation to the others with whom they work. The few unscrupulous should not be given ambiguity to exploit. The alternative to a structure that is clear is that confused or politically manipulative people will bring every problem to the highest available level or, dubiously motivated, fail to bring important matters to your attention at all.

2. Staff the structure carefully. People animate structure. They can also vitiate it, particularly when it is new. Bad personnel decisions are expensive and this is an area where mistakes are frequently made.

Good personnel decisions require time, thought, intuition and sound judgment. Alfred Sloan, the CEO at General Motors who is credited with having saved the company in its infancy, was a decisive man who took his time when making important hiring decisions, because he had learned that his first inclination was usually wrong. Jack Welsh, Chairman and CEO of General Electric, makes a similar point. Telephone conversations with friends which ask them implicitly to support one's already formed opinion will not suffice to choose the lateral partner who is going to head up your new intellectual property group.

T.S. Eliot was asked if he had had second thoughts after writing the first draft of his poem, "The Waste Land." Eliot replied, "All my thoughts are second thoughts." Don't be embarrassed that you are no more prescient than the great poet. This year, 2022, is the one hundredth anniversary of his great poem.

Be alert to the ethnic, gender, and age demography in your firm and be aware of the patterns that are inadvertently created when you hire and promote people. Notice if there are no women on the executive committee, people under 45, or minority members among your equity partners. Keep it in mind; ask yourself why this is the case and how it matters to the quality of decision-making, marketing and client relations, recruitment and retention of associates.

Members of all-male groups without an external enemy to fight can become unmanageably competitive and bitterly rivalrous with one another. The competition may be overt and explosive or covert and erosive or both. At the same time, do not promote or assign leadership roles primarily on the basis of demographic qualification. This is a recipe for failure and lawsuits.

3. Do not violate you own structure. If you want structure to work, you must act in conformity with it. If you don't, few others will. Structure that does not have the solidity of tradition requires conscious observation until practice becomes habitual. In an organization this is more likely to be matter of years (but not decades) than of months. In a nation, decades may be required. This is why "nation building" by people with short attention spans (i.e., us) fail. The point is not that organizational structure should never be circumvented, but that you need to be mindful of the potential costs of doing so. If you find that there is no good way to do something that needs to be done within the

existing structure and the problem recurs, then a change in structure is needed.

4. Respect group boundaries and the authority of their leaders to manage them. If chaos involves not knowing who or what belongs where, then well-managed boundaries are essential to sanity and the orderly conduct of business. For example, if you have created practice groups each with its own head, do not bypass them to intervene directly with one of their members. When an associate tells you of having trouble with a senior partner, for example, do not intervene directly but instead refer the matter to the leader of the practice group.

Beware of good values rationalizations, the noble thoughts that spring to mind to rationalize doing something that you want to do but know you shouldn't. Be aware that decent people such as yourself usually require good reasons to do bad things. In the above example, you decide to go directly to the senior partner (with whom you've been annoyed for years) to confront him. The good values rationalization is that it is unfair to ask the practice group leader to deal with the senior partner, because he is too junior. "Walking the halls" offers itself here as another good values rationalization for meddling in other people's departments.

What you will have done is diminished the practice group leader's authority by reinforcing the idea that the senior partner is accountable only to you. You will have robbed the young practice group leader of the opportunity to take a step forward in establishing his leadership of the group.

In general, you should discourage reports, formal and informal, from people who do not report directly to you. Turn a deaf ear to the "Open Door Policy" good values rationalization that offers itself to justify your imitation of the Statue of Liberty. As noted, accepting such reports undermines the authority of managers beneath you and vitiates the structure that is the chief protection against the unbridled effects of personality and its deformations. Done often, it will bring out the worst in people, creating a culture of gossip, intrigue and prurience, not to mention petty and mean-spirited advantage seeking. Remember it is the unscrupulous who prosper in the interstices of structure; the well intentioned find little appeal in them.

The executives who fall victim to illusions of omnipotence are the same ones who complain bitterly that their managers are too passive and that they have to do everything. When you are doing the work of a department head or practice group leader or executive director, or indulging in a Statue of Libertyesque rescue of a staff member, no one is leading the firm. If your marketplace is Edenic, this may not matter much. If it is competitive and unforgiving, it may be a fateful abnegation of responsibility.

5. Do not create groups and committees willy-nilly. Other things being equal, it is better to assign a new task to an existing committee than to create a new one. Why? Because we are trying to keep the structure as simple as possible so that people are clearheaded about their responsibilities. Every new standing committee constitutes a change in the structure and will require integration with other, already existing groups. Without integration, the activity of one group can act as a constraint upon the work of another. For example, a new committee on mentoring is created which resolves to require 50 hours per year from each partner while a compensation committee has decided to increase the weight given to originations.

Individuals with too many committee assignments—say, more than two—tend to show up irregularly or to do so in a vacant attitude, participating little in the work of the group. Worse, they may be mindlessly obstructive; for example, insisting that the group revisit decisions previously made in their absence.

Committees so formed work poorly and contribute to the prevailing cynicism about committees, which then makes it hard to use one when you really need to.

When problems arise, try thinking first about structure rather than about persons. If, for example, two partners come to you with a dispute about sharing billing credit, resist the inclination to blame one of them. Problematic personalities over-react to organizational problems but are rarely their cause. Consider instead whether there isn't something wrong with the compensation system, or in the concept of, or procedure for, assigning billing credit. If there are people at an intermediate level of authority, ask yourself whether you ought to be meeting with these partners at all. The answer is usually "No."

6. Do not allow groups to be co-led. As Ohio State Football Coach Woody Hayes once said about the forward pass, three things can happen, and two of them are bad.

a. The co-leaders will divide the labor and authority between them explicitly and in a task effective manner. (If you believe this will happen, I have a bridge over the East River in New York for sale I'd like to talk to you about).

b. Each co-leader will assume that the other will take responsibility for leading the work and each will return to business as usual while the task languishes.

c. Both co-leaders will move forward with minimal coordination, creating duplication of effort, contradictory information to colleagues and frustrating multiple subordination of assistants. The job will be botched and responsibility for the failure diffused.

If you are serious about an assignment, give it to one person to perform either individually or in his or her capacity as leader of a group. Having delegated a task to an individual, neither disappear nor meddle, but maintain a consistent, persistent, light but not insubstantial supervisory hand on the matter: e.g., "How are things going with the such and such?"

7. Assign roles to the right positions and clarify their relative priority. For example, if the position Director of Professional Training (DPT) exists within your structure, and it occurs to you that someone should head a mentoring program, you need good reasons why this new role should not be assigned to the DPT.

But what if you don't have much confidence in your DPT? Wouldn't it be smarter to create a new position? No, because this institutionalizes the problem. It converts a personnel problem into a structural one. Supervise the DPT or get him coaching or replace him.

Sizeable law firms typically have several marginally competent people who have become refugee members of the staff, the essential aspects of whose roles have been assigned to others. They are identifiable by their greasy, apologetic smiles and distinguishable from associates by their advanced age. Their primary contribution appears to be as symbols of the firm's kindness and tolerance for human frailty. Typically, they don't cost much and, in any event, are quickly dispatched with each change of administration.

A person occupies one position in an organization and from that position performs multiple roles. Confusion ensues if you imagine that each role constitutes a separate position or that the concrete acts engaged in constitute separate roles. For example, the position of President of the United States has traditionally carried the three roles of head of the executive branch of government, commander and chief of the armed forces, and leader of his political party. Leading cabinet meetings is not a separate role but rather one of the activities the president engages in in his role as head of the executive branch of government.

The confusion of roles and activities renders job descriptions useless, if not actually disorganizing. A long list of activities provides no conceptual order and no indication of priority. Who but a masochist or a sloppy worker would accept responsibility for doing too many things?

Positions rarely carry more than three roles; if you think one does, you have not thought through the position sufficiently to identify its essential functions.

Here is a grocery shopper's job description: buy milk, butter, cheese, steak, veal, chicken, sword fish, salmon, lettuce, tomatoes, onions, avocados, grapes, figs, oranges, melon....

Here is a grocery shopper's role properly conceived. Shop for groceries: buy dairy products, meat, vegetables and fruit.

8. Name positions in such a way that the title indicates the incumbent's authority and relationship to the task. Ask yourself, "Would a client be able to tell what this person does from his or her title?" Would the person who holds it? Roles have an "ought" quality and responsible people internalize the requirements as well as the attendant imagery. If you make someone "President," he or she will feel some obligation to behave in a presidential manner and be affronted when his authority is not recognized.

Avoid giving the title of "Director" to someone who has no one to direct but himself and his assistant.

Companies often employ the language of "Senior Vice President," "Executive Vice President," and "Vice President" and award these titles lavishly to multiple individuals. "Vice President" indicates a number two level of authority and back-up responsibility to a number one. Creating three grades of number two and arraying these across several individuals makes a structure overly complex and asks people to observe distinctions that are too small.

9. Watch the connotative meanings of your management language and the imagery it evokes. This is a delicate matter, because attorneys rightfully pride themselves on their verbal ability. Yet even when used by the articulate, words can communicate unintended meanings that provoke unexpected reactions. For example, to call the laying off of partners and associates a "reduction in force" sounds impersonal and makes the managing partner seem callous. It also suggests that he imagines himself to be a military leader. Both are stimulants to rebellion.

To refer to your executive committee as "Ex Com" is to evoke the imagery of the CIA and support the belief, common in law firms, that management pursues its own purposes in secret. Don't be surprised by partners' cynicism about your intentions and procedures.

Do not title any *ad hoc* committee a "task force" unless you intend it to engage in armed attack upon a competing law firm. Partners assigned to a task force on the recruitment of summer clerks are likely to feel ridiculous.

To call a practice group leader a "Piggle" (PGL), renders him or her a chubby cartoon character with no authority. Group members may treat him as such.

If the "Mentoring Partner's" primary responsibility is to gather supervisory evaluations and join in presenting them to associates, he is not a mentor but a coordinating supervisor. The title inflates hopes, the performance disappoints accordingly.

You can't call partners "Timekeepers" on Monday and complain on Tuesday that they act like employees rather than owners. They will resent you for both.

The title "Executive Director," commonly used to identify the head of administration, packs an authority punch in both words. It overstates grandly the authority actually given to the position, since the executive director is subordinate to the managing partner, executive committee members, and, too often, every other partner as well. He or she is set up to feel like a fraud or a failure and to be the target of acting out by administrative subordinates. If the executive director acts puffy and officious think about how you have structured and named the role rather than about his childhood.

10. Name groups logically. Do not, for example, create a merger and acquisition *group* within the corporate practice group, because it obscures which is the whole and which is a part and blurs priority and accountability. Instead, call it a team.

More correctly, a program may be undertaken or a team formed by a group, one or more groups will fit within a department; one or more departments will operate comfortably within a division; one or more divisions may make up a center or a company and so on.

Isn't this just semantics? No, it matters to the clear-headed sense of responsibility we are hoping to bring out in colleagues and subordinates. We want people to know where they are in the structure and the responsibility they carry for the tasks of the various groups within it.

Recognize that an automatic process of memorization occurs as we speak and write. The words we use expressively come to be the words with which we think. Calling things by the wrong names comes in time to blur reality and make it hard to grasp. We end up viewing our roles and the organization and its challenges through a miasma of cliché and malapropism and render ourselves incompetent—not as attorneys but as managers.

A facilitating structure is a manager's best friend. Build, staff, and manage it competently, including calling things by their right names, and you will find yourself freed to think creatively and lead rather than constrained simply to cleaning up after the circus.

4. Managing Through a Recession: The Case of Bright Star Technology, Int.

Janet is ready to quit. She is production manager in the Seattle office of Bright Star Technology, Int., a computer company headquartered in Tokyo. Her assistant, Becky, is driving her nuts. Whenever she tells Becky that "they" ought to do something, like check on the status of a part that had been ordered, Becky replies, "You're right; you should do that," as though she were giving Janet a directive. Becky also has the maddening tendency to tell her supervisor in front of others that she is "wrong," whenever she disagrees with her, even when her agreement is not being sought. Janet has confronted her with this odd behavior on multiple occasions, for a long time in a friendly manner and more recently with direct requests that Becky stop it. Janet told Becky that if she has an important disagreement, she should take it up with her in private.

Alarmed at the prospect of Janet leaving, Edward, the CEO, asked me to coach her to find more effective ways of supervising her assistant.

The production manager was not the only person whom Becky treated in this way. The warehouse manager, who, like Janet, had been with the company for over a decade, was also given these same instructions, but he dealt with them differently. He stopped Becky before she finished her sentence, insisting that he be allowed to speak. Both the production manager and the warehouse manager were a full generation older than Becky, so it appeared that Becky might be accepting his authority because he was male.

In her late 30s, Becky had risen from the shop floor of the company because of her hard work and remarkable memory for detail. Whenever a question came up about the inventory of any part of the company's product, she could be counted upon to know the answer. Janet was less good on the details and had come to rely upon her assistant for her mastery of these matters. Janet's strength was in her sound management judgment, especially when it came to dealing with important clients and with the parent company. A tactful and discrete person, Janet was also the one person to whom other managers could talk about the stresses they experienced in work and sometimes at home.

Leadership Change in The Parent Company

Bright Star Technology's sales had been badly hurt in the recession of 2008.

Sales of their main product had declined 30% over the past two years and had yet to show signs of improvement. The company itself was owned by a wealthy Japanese family who treated it more as an advertisement for their political power than as a commercial enterprise. Recently, the founder had placed the firm under the control of his oldest son, Jason, who was young and had no business experience. Jason immediately moved to extend his control over the Seattle office by demanding detailed reports of all operations and placing customer relations and marketing under his own personal direction.

The CEO of The Seattle Branch Office

Edward, the CEO, had been placed in a humiliating position. At times, Jason bypassed him and dealt directly with his managers, including Janet. At other times, Edward had become impatient with Janet's lack of immediate knowledge of inventory details, and he, too, had taken to going directly to Becky when Tokyo demanded answers. Edward had done so once in a meeting where all those in attendance but Becky were at a manager or director level. This constituted a public act of disrespect for Janet, about which she confronted him later in private. Edward responded defensively, insisting that she was wrong not to know all the facts he needed. Most recently, he had sent out an important memo to his managers and included Becky in the list. No other manager's assistant was included in the distribution and no explanation was given for her inclusion.

Organizational Mirroring

Dysfunctional patterns at the top of the organization were reflected at lower levels; i.e., what the president did to his CEO, his CEO did to his production manager. When Jason bypassed Edward, Janet had been careful to put Edward back into an intermediary position between herself and Tokyo. Becky had not yet learned to do that when Edward bypassed Janet.

The Table of Organization

The table of organization of the Seattle office was telling. It showed boxes of functions; there was one for sales, another for production, a third for marketing and so on. No lines connected the boxes and no positions existed that identified who had responsibility for which function. Although each function or department actually had a director, their positions did not appear on the chart and their relations with each other, on the chart or in actual practice, were unspecified. This table of organization depicted an office in which activity was everything, however disorganized. The chart seemed to say, "What does it matter who's in charge, or how you should work together, hurry up and finish the job."

In practice, all of the managers, including Janet, worked long hours, in part because of the errors resulting from the diffusion of responsibility and duplication of effort. Some part of each day was spent correcting mistakes in sales, or production, or distribution, or purchasing, or reports submitted to Tokyo. Rather than using such mistakes as opportunities to improve organizational structure and learn how to be more efficient, they were used to support attacks among managers as to who was wrong.

The failure to appreciate the importance of structure led, as it typically does, to moralism—the blaming of problems on individuals.

A Culture of Blame

Thus, a culture of accusation and blame existed where a culture of learning and development was needed. This is commonly the case in organizations that are functioning poorly, including American ones. Unlike in Japan, however, in the US failed American CEO's can often look forward to splendid severances and a bright future. This may reflect the Christian value on redemption.

Blaming was unusually strong in this firm because of the importance in Japanese culture of saving face. Individuals felt being wrong to be nearly intolerable and were quick to assign responsibility to others. Interestingly, Janet was the only manager who could stand to be "wrong," and frequently offered to take responsibility for a mistake in order to move discussion forward to find a solution. From peers and superordinate, this was acceptable. From her assistant, it was not.

Weighing The Causes of Becky's Behavior

How do we account for Becky's insubordination? Clearly, there is a personality problem. Her behavior is rigid, repetitive, compulsive. She herself acknowledges the existence of a problem but has difficulty changing her behavior. On occasion, when confronted, she reports convincingly that she is not aware of having just contradicted or issued a directive to her supervisor. Thus, at times, her behavior is unconscious and beyond her control. Note that were our explanation to stop with her personality, we would leave unexplained why Becky's behavior has only become truly problematic in the past year.

Becoming One's Own Woman

Age and career ambition are a factor. At 36, Becky is in the culminating period of early adulthood. She is entering into the developmental phase we call Becoming One's Own Woman, a distinctive phenomenon occurring in the late 30s (Becoming One's Own Man for males). Becky wants to function more independently, speak with her own voice, have some real authority, and gain entrance to the leadership group of her company. Her lack of grace in this pursuit is caused in part by professional insecurity. She does not have a college education and it shows in her speech. Becky has not been allowed to interact directly with important clients for this reason. In a sense, her command of the technical details of production is her B.S. degree, and she asserts it with stubborn determination.

Women In Authority

There is also the issue of authority relations between women. My research with my colleague Marjorie Bayes on women in authority, published in 1978 and reprinted in the *Conference Board*, analyzed the difficulty some women have accepting the authority of a woman in circumstances where they will do so with a man. Note the relative ease with which the warehouse manager succeeds in stopping Becky. At the same time, Bayes and I found that women supervisors can be slow to exercise their authority directly, bending over backward to be friendly and patient with a recalcitrant subordinate. This had been the case with Janet.

Gender and age interact here, as the full generational difference between Janet and Becky may evoke a mother-daughter style of authority relation in which dismissal is unthinkable and cannot operate as a sane-making constraint. Instead, bad behavior and 'parental' admonition go on as though potentially interminable. That a mother might fire her daughter is inconceivable.

Systemic Factors

These personal and interpersonal factors account for only part of the problem. What accounts for the rest? These other factors are, in order of importance; 1) The Recessionary Environment: declining sales have led to leadership changes in the parent company; 2) System Leadership: the new president violates the boundary of his branch office; 3) President-CEO Working Relationship: Jason makes no attempt to work with Edward to solve the problem of diminished revenue, but instead, acting from a 4) Firm-Wide Culture Of Blame demands that his CEO produce justificatory data as though under subpoena. 5) Structure Violating Delegation: humiliated and angry, Edward seeks to comply with Tokyo's demands while involving himself as little as possible. Turning directly to Becky serves this defensive purpose but elevates the status of the detail-oriented assistant, and stimulates her inappropriate behavior toward Janet.

The systemic factors lead to Becky's regression and acting out. Janet's attempts to supervise Becky correctively are nullified by direct requests for information from Edward. Unconsciously, Becky may feel like father's favorite, an untouchable princess. If so, it would be ironic, since this regressive gratification would defeat her efforts to acquire more authority as an adult.

Coaching Janet

Janet is an important member of the management of the Seattle office and, indeed, of the company as a whole. They cannot afford to have her quit. She is the only person who has succeeded in maintaining good relations with important clients, Seattle branch office management, and Tokyo. Becky is valuable, too.

As Janet learns more about the systemic sources of Becky's behavior, she is better able to respond evenly with direct correctives. Nonetheless, as long as Edward keeps violating his own office structure with direct appeals to Becky for information, it will be hard for the assistant to sustain improvement. Edward and I have begun conversations about his contribution to the problem between Becky and Janet.

Leadership Strength

It is precisely under conditions of this sort that the leadership strength of a manager shows itself. As we saw in the earlier material on leaders and followers, control of the external boundary is necessary for system integrity. Thus, it is the primary requirement of leadership. Jason's interventions violate this boundary, undermine Edward's authority, and disorganize the branch office.

It would be understandable if Edward drinks excessively, becomes short-tempered with his wife and children, develops a stress related illness, or quits. Should he leave, the *Dauphin* in Tokyo would quickly learn that he does not really know how to run this business and, in any event, cannot do so directly from Tokyo. Important clients in the US will drop away when the people they have learned to trust in Seattle have left the office.

But as long as Edward stays in the position of CEO, he must do what he can to protect and improve its structure. Helping Edward deal with Tokyo has become part of an expanded coaching engagement.

Chapter Five
Structuring and Managing Compensation

1. Toward a Saner Compensation System: The Case of Sigmo, Ido & Scopy, LLP

Law firm compensation systems are a perennial source of wounded pride, corrosive anger, and residual bitterness. Even when great care is devoted to arriving at a fair distribution of profits, the perception of personal factors at work and the sense of illegitimacy are rife.

Further, anxieties, disappointments and resentments from other aspects of work and personal life are displaced and focused upon the compensation system and those who administer it. Law firms abound with otherwise healthy persons who suffer from PCTSD (Post-Compensation Traumatic Stress Disorder), a condition from which the chances of full recovery appear to be poor, despite the abiding affluence of its victims.

At the full service Chicago firm of Sygmo, Ido & Scopy, LLP compensation decisions are made in the following way: Yearly, every partner evaluates his own and every other partner's performance and each submits recommendations to a committee; the managing partner interviews each partner individually; the committee meets multiple times and, together, with the managing partner, makes recommendations to the partnership about the distribution of profits; and, but not finally, there is discussion and voting by the entire partnership. Finally, there are appeals from partners, typically about 20% in any given year. At a conservative estimate, the cost to the firm in man and woman hours is about $500,000 and the attention of the managing partner is consumed for the first two months of every year.

What are the results? Typically, there is little change in the previous year's compensation of most partners. Those who receive less than they believe right have had their relations with their peers contaminated by the diffusion of responsibility for the decision. They threaten to take calls from headhunters and are left spoiling for a fight.

This is a distinctive feature of law firms. The preoccupation with compensation and the expense incurred in setting it is not shared by other commercial enterprises or by most professional service organizations. Interviewing an attorney, one doesn't wait long before hearing of a compensation enormity. Some of these outrages have occurred as many as ten or twenty years prior, yet the wound remains open and the outrage fresh. Interviewing other professionals, the matter rarely comes up.

Are attorneys more materialistic than doctors, professors, and executive vice presidents in business? My experience in consulting to members of all of these groups leads me to say that the answer is "No." Are attorneys pettier than their counterparts in hospitals, universities, and commercial enterprises: Again, my answer is "No."

Viewing the annual regression into greed and envy, lawyers conclude that it is simply human nature at work. Yet as was discussed in Chapter One, human nature has more than one side, and it is the responsibility of firm leaders to create structures that bring out the best in people. The absence of a rational system for making salary determinations and the failure to invest authority in managers to do so works an indignity on attorneys and reduces some to the condition of hateful children—a further indignity.

Politics Over Commerce

The historical tendency in the leadership of law firms is from a patriarchy of founders to a band of brothers and sisters who create a management structure designed to prevent tyranny. Fearful of a return to autocracy and nepotism, the 'siblings' use the democratic polity as a model for determining firm organizational structure; so, questions of constituency, representation, coalition and appeal reign, while those of efficiency, managerial competence, authority and responsibility are neglected. Yet, as has been noted, the law firm is a commercial enterprise not a political entity.

If one sets up a system along political lines, it will be politicized. Further, one cannot politicize organizational life without making it rancorous.

A rational next step in the evolution of the law firm requires the creation of a structure for responsible management in which leaders are authorized to deal efficiently with compensation and other important matters. This means investing real authority in the role of managing partner and allowing him to appoint his own executive committee under the oversight of an elected board of which the managing partner is a nonvoting member. If the firm is other than very small, there should be department heads and or practice group leaders. The managing partner should appoint these, and they must have real influence in decisions about compensation and other matters.

Compensation in such firms could be accomplished in a fraction of the time now required and with far less rancor. Indeed, in one comparable firm, which accepted and implemented these recommendations, the managing partner and his executive committee make these decisions in a single day. Firm morale is better in this firm than at Sigmo, Ido & Scopy, even though profits per partner are lower due to lower rates in their marketplace. Unhappiness about perceived inequities is mild and infrequent; and, what there is, partners direct at the managing partner, rather than at their peers.

By and large, partners leave politics at the door. Further, since adopting this management structure, the firm's revenues have steadily and significantly increased during good economic times and bad while those of Sigmo, Ido & Scopy have not.

In subsequent sections of this chapter, I will describe the advantages and disadvantages of the several usual approaches to compensation—equal distribution, seniority, and formula—and discuss further the operational principles that should underlie the choice.

Some readers will be surprised to find emphasized the several advantages of the seniority approach, which had been relegated to the dust bin of law firm history. Let me assure the skeptical reader that I recognized the organizational significance of these advantages while I was still young.

2. Toward a Saner Compensation System

Jim is the managing partner of a mid-sized Phoenix firm. It is seven a.m. on March 1. He looks like he just got back from Iraq. His hair looks ratty, and his eyes bulge. There are holes in his shirt and smoke seems to be rising from his open collar. "Well, it's all done, except for the appeals," he tells me. The slate of compensation and bonus assignments has been approved for another year.

It took two months and has cost over $350,000 in man and woman hours with more expense to come in order to deal with the expectable appeals. The attachment of some partners to the firm has been strained and a few carry a residue of personal bitterness whose half-life will extend to the grave.

Surely, there is a better way.

Equal Pay

The evolution of compensation systems in U.S. law firms has tended to evolve from equal pay to seniority to formula then to subjective systems like Jim's, although failed and successful examples of each form still exist.

The equal pay system worked well in firms that were small but was felt to be problematic as firms grew. The team spirit advantage of the approach diminished as differential productivity among partners increased. Should a partner billing two-thirds the hours of another receive the same compensation? Is it equitable that a partner whose collections are twice that of another be compensated at the same level? Ought a new partner be paid the same as one who has been a partner for twenty years?

Seniority

In part as a reaction to such inequities, some firms came to adopt seniority as the central criterion in their compensation system. Years with the firm had the advantage of rewarding both loyalty and productivity, since the correlation between experience and collections is high. The objective, orderly, and public nature of seniority as a criterion left attorneys free to concentrate on their work. It was also simple to administer and it limited the contamination of peer relations by competition for favor. As the size of law firms grew and the legal marketplace became more competitive, encouraged by consultants to become more entrepreneurial, firms moved away from seniority systems, dismissing them as "lockstep."

Yet there are advantages to an emphasis upon seniority. As mentioned, it rewards loyalty and provides predictability. It also limits personal embarrassment, offers ease and economy of administration, and reinvests pride and ambition from compensation into work.

These advantages are sufficient to warrant serious consideration of making seniority central among the criteria that now are typically used to determine compensation. Outstanding achievement of junior partners could be handled through bonus allocations. Indeed, as a modest proposal, perhaps bonuses ought to be awarded primarily to junior partners, on the grounds that they may need them.

Avoiding generational warfare. The seniority system has further advantages, significant even though intangible. It eases relations among the generations by lessening the competition among them. Reducing competition promotes mentoring. It allows marketing responsibilities to settle where they most naturally would reside—upon the established— and facilitates the movement of work from above to below. By contrast, a system based primarily upon production creates a Hobbsean "war of all against all' where only a fragile civility is possible when a truer partnership is wanted.

A culture of honor. Seniority is a compensation criterion in which honor is bestowed as an earned reward for age. Older partners can enjoy it and younger ones can look forward to it. Honoring the old encourages seniors to allow the leadership generation of attorneys in their 40s and 50s to lead, since the seniors do not feel unimportant. Relieved of the necessity to protect their authority from above, the leadership generation in the firm is freed to counsel the young lawyers below. Support from above frees the middle generation of attorneys to mentor young lawyers. The antithesis of a law firm culture of honor is one in which everyone is reduced to the level of a "timekeeper," a fungible commodity, where the most accomplished must seek to hold on to power beyond their time.

The archetype of the Slothful Partner. The primary disadvantage of the seniority approach is that a senior attorney might retire without telling anyone. It would then fall to the managing partner to confront the delinquent. Many managing partners do not feel up to this task. Typically, the managing partner is a half-generation younger than the delinquent senior; worse, the oldster may once have been the managing partner's mentor. Disastrously, the senior might end up on a committee formed to determine the managing partner's bonus.

Similarly, it is popularly imagined that many tenured professors are wankers. In fact, the data show that tenured professors continue to out-publish their untenured colleagues. The main reason for this is not unlike the reason for the greater productivity of senior lawyers vis-à-vis their juniors. Senior people get more invitations to do work—publish books or handle important legal matters—because they are better known and known by those who are better placed to refer good work.

Is it possible that the slothful partner exists primarily as a psychological *archetype*—a preformed readiness to experience something—like Big Foot or a grateful child? Could the slothful partner achieve its regnant persistence not so much through actual experience as through the collective projections of exhausted attorneys longing for a break? Is it a specter created first through a renounced wish—"*I* do not want to be lazy"—and second through a projection—"*he* wants to be lazy?"

Nonetheless, it might occasionally fall to a managing partner to have an unpleasant conversation with a senior who has become underproductive because of declining health or a descent into voluptuousness. An effective response to the first might require the managing partner to master his guilt; to the second, his envy.

Formula

Fearful of these situations and despite, as attorneys, knowing better, some firms moved to create a system for all that would deter the possible deviance of a few. Relieving the managing partner of potentially distasteful responsibilities, compensation decisions would be determined by a formula.

The formula approach promised to eliminate the personal exercise of authority entirely. In practice, removing the managing partner's responsibility to confront delinquency removed the rest of his authority as well. With no role in compensation decisions, the managing partner ended up with little authority regarding anything else. Computers were running law firms, but some formulas became so complex that the computers needed help. More about this in the Part 3, when we consider the case of "The Secret Committee and the Compensation Lady."

3. Toward a Saner Compensation System: The Bonus Delirium and Reaction Formations

By virtue of established levels, percentages, or points, the main component of law firm compensation does not change dramatically from year to year. The changes that do occur are objective, being based upon how well the firm as a whole did in the previous year. By contrast, decisions about the awarding of bonuses can seem arbitrary and be incendiary.

Despite the fact that 90% or more of a partner's compensation is set and ample, the idea of the bonus creates Christmas Day expectations. As has been said, it is not so much that we grow up, as that our toys get more expensive. For example, an attorney thinks: "I have worked very hard and had a good year. The firm as a whole has had a good year. I am driving an Audi that is three years old. I like the car. It is comfortable, fast and stylish. A 100K bonus would allow me to buy a new Mercedes. I prefer the Mercedes; it looks more impressive than the Audi and is probably more comfortable. The black one looks especially classy." The attorney enlists her husband in the fantasy of a fine new car. "Can we buy it the day after Christmas," he asks? "Why not?" she says.

Now comes the announcement of her bonus. She is excited and then crushed to see that she has been given 30K—enough for a fully loaded Honda Civic. Somehow the fact that she is making 600K a year without the bonus does not help; she thinks, *"How could they do this to me?"*

The disappointment is worsened by the fact that here mummy and daddy are more like brother and sister in age. While mum and dad might disappoint, they rarely do so for bad reasons. By contrast, siblings with power are notoriously villainous. To be slighted by equals is the more hurtful, when one had wanted to think of them as friends, or at least peers, who understood one's situation.

Take Superfluous People Out of the Decision-Making

In a San Diego firm where the dark clouds of partner suspicion never parted for long, a formula was created to handle bonus decisions. The people who derived and entered the numbers were partners chosen by secret ballot. A bookkeeper, who lived in another city, administered and tallied the ballots and notified each partner of his or her accession to "The Secret Committee." These assignments were kept strictly confidential. She also scheduled the meetings, which were held after hours and off-site in a location disclosed only to the elected.

Over the years, the formula had been refined and tweaked to redress some of the noisier complaints until finally it became so mathematically rococo that no partner whom I interviewed understood it.

In time, I got to interview the bookkeeper and asked her, "Who decides who gets what bonus?" She said, "I do." "Who are you," I asked? She blushed brightly and replied, "I'm the Compensation Lady!"

Fantastic? No, true and a practice carried out in an otherwise fine and reputable firm.

More common is the labor intensive, highly scrupulous and public effort that I have described earlier in this chapter. This approach does not work as well as one might hope. When the smoke clears in March, one is surprised at the number of casualties. Appeals arise which will use up a good part of a third month. The unappeased survive their injuries and remain in the ranks yet are left spoiling for trouble. Meanwhile, the managing partner and the department heads are nearly as alienated by the experience as are the aggrieved partners. A dark view of human nature arises on both sides to explain the unseemly disagreements.

Villainy and greed are certainly human, but not as common as psychological defense mechanisms. We all rely upon these every day.

The Obsessive Compulsive Defense of Reaction Formation

Here we must enter the dark realm of unconscious psychology where we encounter, among others, a defense mechanism called *reaction formation*. Freud first discovered this mechanism nearly 100 years ago in his treatment of a young man—an attorney as it happened—who was obsessed by fears that his sweetheart and his father would be injured. Freud learned that the young man had resented his father and was mad at his fiancé for delaying their marriage and his sexual gratification. In imagining their injury, the man expressed in disguised form his hidden resentment toward his father, who was in fact deceased, and his frustrating girlfriend.

136

Good people, and we are talking about good people, cannot do bad things for other than good reasons. Through reaction formations we adopt the blameless feeling, attitude, state of mind or behavior that is exactly the opposite of our unconscious bad intention.

If we are a touch homicidal, we sell life insurance; if we want to hurt a patient, we cleanse his wound until it is raw. If we are inclined to punish our peers, we carry out the allocation of their bonuses so assiduously as to leave them bepretzeled. We invest so much personal consideration in the decision that they take it very personally. In the name of fairness, we carry out as much of this as possible publicly; thus, do we succeed in humiliating those who receive less than they believe their due by trumpeting their inferiority.

Reaction formations are the preeminent defense mechanism in obsessive compulsive personalities, which he found in Chapter One to be modal in the law firm. They are the defense mechanism of the scrupulous and well intentioned; that is to say, you and I. Indeed, it is our scrupulosity, not our bad intentions, that gives rise to the reaction formation. Our bad intentions are small beer amidst the enormities of human evil. It is our consciences that mark us; they are so touchy that we find bad wishes intolerable.

The irony is that by trying so hard to avoid doing something wrong we inflict more damage than we might have done had we been able to tolerate the possibility of doing a little.

It is difficult for attorneys with divided minds to think well about their compensation systems. It is also hard for consultants to point out problems without causing the managing partner to feel defensive. Here as elsewhere what is needed is the relaxed and flexible thinking that expands awareness and enhances perspective.

Chapter Six: Boards

1. Boards of Directors

Boards can be dangerous creatures. Intended to provide oversight and long range planning, they can turn out to be agents of disorganization and irresponsibility. Public companies are required to have boards. Some private companies create them to provide additional governance strength. In either case, little thought typically goes into building the relationship between board and management. A similar absence of serious thought is given to the structure and leadership of the board itself.

Relation of Boards to Firm Management

The requirements under Sarbanes-Oxley for independent auditing committees within public company boards hardly simplify the board-management relationship. However necessary for the protection of shareholders' investments, in the group dynamics of this arrangement it is as though a foreign body—or an investigatory agency of the federal government—had been established on the boundary of the company itself. This adds a further complication to an already problematic relationship between firm management and board.

Even among professional service firms not required to have boards, some create them. In one Los Angeles law firm, in addition to a managing partner and his executive committee and department heads, the partners decided that it would be good to have an advisory committee of some eight elected partners. Why? To focus upon policy and long range planning.

Who could object? Managers, as well as the rest of us, can always profit from good advice. Eight heads are better than one and so on. Why eight? Because six seemed too few to be representative (sic) and ten larger than necessary.

What was the primary task of the committee? To give advice. To whom? Well, to the managing partner. Did he want advice provided in so collective, formal and public a manner? Could he use it? These questions were never asked. Nor was the possibility envisioned that board members with vague responsibilities and uncertain authority might become anxious and blame the managing partner for their incompetence. Responsible people on a board are likely to feel that they ought to do something.

Authority Problems

Who was to head the advisory committee? No one knew. Facing this question might have exposed the illusion that the board would not exercise authority but simply give advice. In practice, it evolved that the head of the committee was its most senior partner with the biggest book of business.

Before long it became apparent that the managing partner would be required to report to the advisory committee. He had in effect been demoted and his role radically changed. De facto, everyone who reported to the managing partner, including the department heads, had been demoted as well.

A year later, the tenure of the managing partner was bloodily discontinued after he and the advisory committee had come to loggerheads. The effects of that acrimonious dispute still linger, strengthening a theme in the firm's history of leadership feeling abused and discarded.

Will qualified junior partners among the emergent leadership generation in the firm be eager to take their turn at bat? Was the authority relationship between board and management resolved or at least clarified in this messy struggle? Or does the stage remain set for future conflict?

Groups are Social Systems

In the pervasive neglect of organizational structure and system dynamics, it is not understood that the creation of a new, major committee is intrinsically de-stabilizing. For it is exactly the interdependence of groups and roles within an organization that distinguishes it from an *aggregate* of activities and persons.

Organizations are social systems and within a system every part influences every other part. To the extent that a law firm is integrated, then to that extent are its major components—groups and roles—interdependent. To the extent that it remains instead an aggregate of solo practitioners or small law firms, then to that extent is money lost through poorly controlled expenses and missed opportunities. There is no desirable alternative to interdependence and integration.

Even though an advisory board may be a good idea, careful attention and sustained effort will have to go into working out the relationship between this committee and others in authority. This means the executive committee, the managing partner and the department heads.

A tinker toy approach in which structures are created and dismantled at will is too costly. Partners must bring the same considered judgment and deliberate action to the functioning of their boards that they bring to the conduct of their legal work.

Board retreats led by facilitators who are expert in system structure and dynamics can help boards organize themselves better and relate more constructively to firm leadership.

In the next section, we will consider the illusions of unadulterated rationality and impartiality to which board members, breathing the heady ether of a *hors de combat* altitude, are vulnerable and their costly consequences.

2. Boards of Directors: The Case of H-P

Most law firms muddle through with little management. Managing partners, often part-time and untrained, wish that they had sufficient authority and help to create enduring solutions to chronic firm problems. They cast envious, admiring glances toward "Corporate America," envisioned as a world in which things are run properly. Consultants make a living warning law firms about the necessity of better management and drawing unfavorable contrasts between the billable hour chasing of the law firm and the efficient rationality of the business world.

The Illusion of Corporate Rationality

It is true that companies of any appreciable size tend to be better managed than law firms. They have full time managers at multiple levels and public companies have boards. But their superiority is relative and sometimes illusory.

Lest there be any doubt about this, we have recently had the instructive spectacle of Hewlett-Packard's Board. The data for this analysis of H-P come from public records, not from a consulting relationship. Evidently, the board hired private investigators to determine the source of "leaks" of their own deliberations. Inspired, perhaps, by investigatory practices now sanctified at the highest levels of the Republic, and following a practice begun by her ousted predecessor, H-P Chairwoman Dunn commissioned an investigation in which not only were board members and employee phone records hacked but those of major newspaper reporters as well.

Apparently, this extreme measure grew out of a longstanding leadership struggle between subgroups within the board. Dunn denies approving the investigators' theft of social security numbers used for 'pretexting'— Orwellian newspeak for lying and impersonation in order to secure phone records—and the matter is currently under investigation by state and federal officials.

The Hewlett-Packard Way

Hewlett-Packard had prided itself on its collegial culture, which in a happier day could be referred to without fear of derision as "the Hewlett-Packard Way." Imagine what the group dynamics are like in boards of companies that do not emphasize collegiality. Indeed, the fact that H-P's stock was unaffected by the scandal suggests that Wall Street considered H-P's board operatics to be unexceptional and little cause for alarm, since company management was not involved. More recently, as CEO Hurd has been implicated, the stock has appeared more vulnerable.

Nonetheless, indictments are in the offing, a shareholder lawsuit has been filed, and an invitation to appear before a congressional committee extended. Ms. Dunn has been removed from the board and replaced by the current CEO, who will function in both capacities. Presumably, Mr. Hurd as CEO will report to himself as Chairman of the Board. This arrangement would seem to institutionalize the leadership problem and compromise the independence of the board. While this arrangement does not violate the letter of Sarbanes-Oxley, it does seem inconsistent with its spirit.

Getting It Wrong by Calling It Wrong

Once again the misnaming of organizational problems contributes to the fiasco. As discussed earlier, what we call things influences how we understand them and understanding guides practice.

Clichés, such as "leaks," are insidiously misleading. These terms are not derived from thoughtful determination of what things actually are and ought to be called, but rather from a set of prefabricated terms that are currently being repeated in the popular culture (newspapers, internet, television, movies, music).

Saturated as we are by media, clichés can be minted quickly. "9/11" became one in a matter of days. Further, as earlier noted, the connotative meaning of words can be as important as the definitional meanings. Indeed, the connotative meanings can be more important motivationally, since they operate upon our feelings at a level outside of conscious awareness.

Ms. Dunn was trying to stop "leaks." What word is strongly associated with "leaks?" *Security*. The term "security leaks" and its shorthand, "leaks," derives from the politico-military world where lives and the future of nations are, presumably, at risk. During WWII it was said with greater justification that "Loose lips sink ships."

Bad Reasons and Bad Music Never Sound as Good as When Marching Against an Enemy

To speak of "leaks" creates an atmosphere of danger and a pretext for recourse to extraordinary means. Having inappropriately inflated the danger of the unapproved publication of H-P Board deliberations—on, say, the introduction of a smaller, cheaper fax/copier/printer—extreme measures followed naturally. The cliché term "weapons of mass destruction" had the same effect on our national leaders regarding Iraq.

Apart from the ethical and legal problems, is it managerially rational for a company to go after The New York Times, The Wall Street Journal, and Business Week by impersonating their reporters to gain access to phone records? Who has more readers—these periodicals or the H-P Quarterly Report? Is it organizationally sound to frighten board members and employees by engaging in practices that trigger investigations by the California State Attorney General, the FBI, the FCC, the SEC, and the House Committee on Energy and Commerce?

One imagines that an organizational analysis of H-P's Board problems would have led to a different, less dramatic characterization and a more temperate intervention strategy.

It would not be surprising if it were found that group problems prior to and consequent of the removal of the previous Chair remained unresolved and found a new victim in Ms. Dunn. Perhaps the "leaks" and the draconian attempts to uncover their source were both symptoms of group problems unresolved by the ousting of her predecessor.

If something of the sort were at work, would not executive coaching for the Chair and team building retreats for the Board have been a more constructive approach?

3. Making Boards Effective

As noted earlier, work groups abound in commercial, academic, and governmental settings. Important, sometimes crucial, tasks are entrusted to committees of all kinds. Standing committees provide an especially important linking device between individual and organization. In a commercial enterprise, where an executive or leadership committee consisting of department heads and a CEO or president exists, the committee links each department member to top management. Individual workers can look to their department heads to carry their concerns upwards to top management, and they can expect their department heads to bring issues of company-wide significance down for their information and discussion.

Even where the requisite structural connections exist, work groups often do not work very well. They do little to achieve organizational goals or to elicit the genuine collaboration of individual members. Their failure adds to the sense of powerlessness of the individual and to the isolation of firm leadership. When collective effort is required, it is discovered that the firm is too poorly integrated to meet a serious challenge. To use a military analogy, a situation obtains in which generals find themselves without armies, and soldiers without leaders. The company has been getting by merely on the talent and hard work of individuals.

Team Building

The difficulty of making groups effective is typically underestimated. Individuals are put together in groups because they work in the same department or are thought to have special interest or competence in the group's task. It is expected that work will get done because the group members are rational adults who are getting paid for their effort. When it is noticed that the group is not accomplishing much and that the problem of ineffective groups is firm-wide, consultants are hired to conduct retreats. Too often the consultants cheapen the problem with entertaining gimmicks like cooking exercises and amateur sail boat races or personality tests that show that people are different. These devices are designed to illustrate some general principle about cooperation in an entertaining manner. Consultants and company leaders collude to avoid the discomfort of confronting problems that exist in their actual work groups.

The problem of building effective groups awaits leaders when they return to the office on Monday. Many do not know how to go about it and fear that the underlying problems are unmanageable. What should they do to help their groups be more effective? Below, I offer six suggestions.

First, work group leaders must define the group's primary task and assert its priority in a persistent and compelling manner. They need to personify the primary task, creating a normative culture—a shared sense about what members ought to be doing and ought not to be doing — that arises from the nature and importance of the task and the leader's devotion to it.

Second, leaders need to look to the composition of the group to make certain that those needed for task achievement are included and superfluous individuals are not.

Third, leaders need to get control of the boundary of the group to obtain necessary inputs and ward off toxic or disorganizing ones. The latter may include the unmonitored intrusion of superordinates.

Fourth, he or she must build the group's structure by clarifying the roles and role relationships of its members.

Fifth, leaders must secure the active, constructive cooperation of followers and help them learn how to talk and listen to each other. Leaders have to actively manage interpersonal problems that interfere with work.

Sixth, and finally, leaders have to monitor the structure and its staffing and make whatever changes prove necessary.

Examples of Effective and Ineffective Groups

All of this takes time and will be most easily achieved in a standing group that meets regularly. Where the group is *ad hoc*, the skill and activity of the leader becomes yet more important.

President Kennedy's use of *ad hoc* committees in both the Bay of Pigs and Cuban Missile Crisis events is instructive. The first committee was weakly led and functioned poorly; the second performed well because it was derived from a standing committee so that relationships did not have to be created from scratch, and because it was very actively led.

It is an anomaly that in the structure of the executive branch of the federal government there is no standing executive or leadership group to help the president make decisions. In the earlier days of the republic, the cabinet could serve this function, because it was small. Washington's cabinet numbered four, Lincoln's seven, FDR's New Deal cabinet eight and Eisenhower's 11. All of these groups were within the permissible size limits of effective work groups. By George W. Bush's presidency, the number had swollen to 20, a number much too large for a group to handle any but the simplest of tasks, such as information sharing. Each of the modern presidents has had to form a leadership group anew with varying degrees of success.

In the Cuban Missile Crisis, Kennedy created a smaller Executive Committee out of the standing National Security Council. By all accounts, the group worked well together. This was in part because at 13 the group was just small enough and because the president delegated the leadership of the committee to Secretary of State Rusk at times, Attorney General Robert Kennedy at others, when he could not be present. Absenting the highest level of authority while maintaining fully authorized, delegated leadership freed discussion by lowering the performance significance of individual contributions. President

Kennedy instructed Rusk and Robert Kennedy to secure full and active participation of all group members, while the president retained responsibility for deciding among their recommendations.

Challenged by their leaders to do so, Executive Committee members argued, sometimes passionately, and people changed their positions, some more than once. To have had a coolly rational discussion about so terrifying a problem could only have occurred if members had denied the dreadful possibilities and repressed their appropriate fear. The rationality thus obtained would have involved the sort of denatured logic that never touches the earth and leads to terrible mistakes when applied.

This sort of active, fully engaged discussion was very different from what took place in the *ad hoc* committee that a green president had formed 17 months earlier. On the fourth day of his presidency, Kennedy had been presented with a plan crafted by the outgoing Eisenhower administration to invade Cuba. Kennedy's put together a group of 18 from the CIA, Departments of State and of Defense and others, as well as his own special advisors. These men worked in plenary and participated according to protocol, with no one beneath the level of department head speaking unless his superior was absent. There obtained in that room, as presidential advisor and Harvard historian Arthur Schlesinger put it, "a curious air of assumed unanimity," as though the decision to invade had already been made elsewhere by some other group. Unconsciously, the group behaved as if Eisenhower were still president, and they were simply implementing his decision. Thus, they unwittingly diminished their authority, abnegated their responsibility, and rendered themselves incompetent. Discussions were polite, rational and orderly and the decisions reached entirely irrational. Reservations were expressed only outside of the meetings.

Evaluating Board Effectiveness

The performance of boards of directors is especially important because their authority and responsibility is so broad, and because most operate without any effective supervision.

Public companies are required to have boards of directors. Many others do so too in order to strengthen governance. How effective are they? To evaluate their effectiveness, we must return to the fundamental question, "What is the primary task of the group; i.e., what is its *raison d'être?*" In a board of directors, the answer is the "two Ps:" the setting of broad company *policy*, such as a strategic business plan, and the monitoring of management *performance,* such as the success of the CEO in executing it. Where the same person fills the roles of board chair and CEO, performance evaluation is confounded. Note that the "two Ps" are interconnected and constitute two parts of a single, unitary task.

If the primary task of a board is to formulate policy and evaluate the success of management in implementing it, how is *their* effectiveness to be judged? The answer is they must do it themselves. Self-evaluation is an especially important responsibility for boards because, to the extent they are comprised of people without operational responsibility, they are *hors d' combat* and vulnerable to illusions of omnirationality. Boards that act on the basis of such illusions may engage in dis-organizing boundary violations by meddling in company personnel matters, colluding with company factions, and otherwise undermining company management.

Using Freud's conception of personality structure, it is as though the board were the superego and management the ego. Freud's superego attacks the ego with unreasonable demands and harsh criticism. In the same way that the ego develops defense mechanisms such as repression (forgetting) and denial (ignoring) to protect itself from this internal attack, management may find ways to hide imperfect performance from itself and from its board.

It is challenging for boards to meet their evaluative obligations *vis-à-vis* management in a collaborative manner. Where board chair and CEO are different people, as should be the case, the necessity of a good working relationship between the two is paramount. Sophisticated coaching can help the pair avoid unnecessary authority struggles and build a genuine working relationship. The achievement of a constructively evaluative relationship between superego and ego is a developmental task for the mature, healthy individual, as well.

Self-Evaluation Methods

To be listed on the New York Stock Exchange a company's board must engage in periodic self-evaluation. While the NYSE recommends that the task be given to a standing board governance and nominating committee, it does not specify further how a board is to go about conducting its evaluation.

How do boards do it? Every which way; how should they do it? It depends. Overseeing a company that is functioning smoothly without important recent change and whose previous evaluation indicated no major areas of concern may simply require a board meeting for discussion. A board that oversees a firm that is grappling with previously identified major issues or which has undergone important changes in composition, structure or leadership needs to devote more time and effort to a systematic review.

In the latter case, the governance committee may begin by administering a detailed questionnaire to committee members to be filled out and returned to an outside consultant who will maintain confidentiality and analyze the responses. The consultant reports the findings to the governance committee, which shares them with each of the other committees for discussion and action. In either case, it is essential that evaluation be periodic and continuing, and that it occur often enough so that the questions raised by evaluation never disappear entirely from the group's consciousness. It is among the responsibilities of leadership to insure this.

Evaluative Categories and Sample Questions

By highlighting key dimensions of effective group performance, a well-designed questionnaire can be an educational tool as well as a data-gathering device. The one I have developed asks 30 questions that are organized and listed under five critical dimensions of work group performance: 1) Leadership, 2) Task Definition, 3) Structure, and 4) Functioning.

Here are some sample questions from each dimension.

1) Leadership: Characterize the committee chair's leadership style. Is it effective? How could it be improved?

2) Task: Is the committee's task clearly defined? If so, is it generally accepted or is there disagreement about what the committee ought to be doing?

3) Structure: Are the responsibilities attendant upon the respective roles of committee members and chair clear? Is the tenure and succession of the chair and of each committee member understood?

4) Functioning: How fully do members participate in the work of the group? Are there interpersonal problems in the group that effect task performance? If so, how are these managed?

Additional questions regarding each dimension flesh out the results.

These questionnaires can be given to committee members and directed at committee functioning or to each board member with reference to the performance of the board as a whole. Either way, the results should provide a basis for dispassionate analysis of board leadership, followership, structure and functioning. This can be done under the temporary direction of a consultant at a board team building retreat or in regular or special board session where the majority of the agenda is devoted to this item. Here again, the consultant who collected and analyzed the data can assure a reasoned approach to understanding it and making choices, if needed, about concrete steps toward improvement.

Chapter Seven
Careers Across the Life Span

No era in the life cycle is easy. Each has a distinct, complicated character, hard to grasp at the beginning, imperfectly understood even at the end. Periodically, we are required to change the structure of our lives, and sometimes even our very selves, in order to meet the challenges posed by our movement up the generational ladder. To these darkling choices, we bring whatever light we can find. As Freud said, consciousness isn't much, but it is all we have.

As described earlier, organizations typically consist of three generations. Each faces different developmental tasks, and needs different things in order to sustain its motivation for work. First is the *Entering Generation* of young lawyers, aged ~23 to 40; next is the *Leadership Generation* of middle-aged attorneys, roughly ~40 to 58; and, lastly there is the *Retiring Generation* of senior lawyers, ~58-.

Though there are individual and cultural divergences from this pattern, as well as very small or highly specialized firms that differ, it is nonetheless typical of law firms in the developed countries and increasingly beyond. This generational structure also characterizes other professional service organizations (e.g., accountancy, medical, academic), where competence matures slowly over long careers. Technology companies like Yahoo begin mainly with young people and then find, when competition increases and profit margins narrow, they have no experienced managers.

The Entering Generation

The *Entering Generation* of young lawyers faces the tasks of becoming competent in the law, establishing its reputation with clients, and finding a balance between a demanding profession and vulnerable personal lives. Often members of this generation have marriages or seek them, have small children or want them, even as the marriages will be buffeted about among competing demands and can only offer constrained satisfactions.

In the early years, the young lawyers need opportunities as well as encouragement and inspiration from mentors. Instead, many receive critical evaluation and indifference. Later, they will want recognition and independence. If they have been cheated of mentors or let down by them, they may also want the satisfaction of depriving the generation behind them of what was denied to themselves.

In their attempts to make partner or find one, or build their book of business as junior partners, the *Entering Generation* is truly in the trenches. Attrition among young lawyers is high and getting worse and lateral moves are common, even though the desirability of the firm across the street may reside mainly in the fact that it is not the one being left.

For most people, the years ~23-40 constitute the most stressful era in the life cycle.

The Leadership Generation

In the middle, resides the *Leadership Generation*. Middle-aged lawyers occupy that portion of the life cycle where a newly descending trajectory of biological vigor that remains nonetheless substantial and a still rising and newly adequate one of leaderly and professional competence meet.

In their personal lives and at work, the middle lawyers encounter the unapologetic assumption that they will manage everything for the well-being of others. They struggle to sustain viable relations with the seniors, respecting their power while resisting their supervision, and toward the young lawyers who look to them for mentoring. In a vise-like parallel, the *Leadership Generation* may also be caught between the young and old in their families with increasing financial responsibilities in both directions. Meanwhile, they must refashion their own youthful dreams lest they stagnate along the path to retirement. Psychological work is required with little time to do it.

The overriding need of the middle lawyers is for appreciation and gratitude. Too often, they are met at home with resentment from spouses and acting out by children, at work by passive aggressive contention and rivalrous devaluation from peers and disdain from seniors.

The Retiring Generation

At the end of the life cycle stands the *Retiring Generation*. Though few senior lawyers are ready for retirement, by the late 50s most have begun to feel its tidal pull.

The seniors have reached the pinnacle of their profession and the apogee of their legal skills. They are experienced, competent, well known and they have the kind of judgment and perspective that only experience can bring. In providing the highest level of legal service, this kind of judgment is as important, sometimes more, than technical skill. Clients know this instinctively and entrust to the senior attorneys matters of the greatest importance.

Since some of their cohorts have reached similar status in their respective fields, the ~60 year-olds form a kind of informal power elite that extends beyond regional and national boundaries. The best business is handed back and forth among them with less need for the sort of demeaning marketing efforts that were necessary 20 years earlier.

With their knowledge and book of business, the ~60 year-olds also form a potential power elite within the law firm. They may or may not still hold positions of formal authority as board chairs, managing partners, or department heads. Even without portfolio, the seniors are feared and respected and granted considerable informal authority. Younger partners come to them for legal advice; members of the *Leadership Generation* worry about their support and approval of management plans and decisions and fear that if they are not compensated lavishly they will leave and take their book of business with them.

Many law firms have at least one senior who has become a rogue partner and cannot be managed.

Certain that they could run things better than the middle lawyers, the seniors fantasize about taking control of their firms. Rivalry among the seniors, and their disinclination to actually dirty their hands in the managerial waters, prevents them from doing so.

The senior lawyers are entering into an era of the life cycle nearly as stressful as that of the young. Their dominant need is for respect, dignity and deference. Too often they encounter derision, sometimes masked as idealization, and avoidance. The developmental task that presses itself upon them is to build a new relationship to their firms that will help them retire.

The first step involves doing the psychological work necessary to loosen the grip of unrealized career fantasies—for example, of transforming the firm through brilliant leadership, becoming a supreme court justice, or amassing great wealth—and coming to terms with the limited nature of their success.

Senior lawyers face the challenge of retirement with even less cultural guidance and wisdom than is available to the *Entering Generation*. Genuine understanding requires both experience *and* perspective yet no one has ever outlived old age.

1. Outplacement Counseling

Many people, including white-collar professionals, found their work disappearing in The Great Recession of 2008-10. Some were summarily laid off; some saw clients disappear and income with it. Most were likely to feel downsized not simply economically, but personally as well. In a culture in which material values predominate, it can be difficult to avoid thinking that one's net worth is one's actual worth.

Except for those few of us who enjoy unblemished psychological health, only two reactions to the shrinkage seem possible: one either reacts in a depressive manner and blames oneself; or, one reacts in a paranoid manner and blames others. The first reaction is more common among people who have been highly successful and the 'violence' associated with it is usually internal—depression, hypertension, increased drinking. Extreme examples of the paranoid reaction sometimes end up on the 6 o'clock news.

The same internal forces that drive hard work attack the self for 'failure.' It is a fiction that people work harder simply in pursuit of larger bonuses. Some do, but in most cases there is an intermediating psychological agency, the superego. We work harder to earn bonuses so that we can feel good about ourselves for being successful—that is, to appease the harsh internal voice of irrational criticism. The appending of a 50K bonus to a 500K salary would otherwise be small beer.

Skadden Arps found a humane and creative approach to the downturn. The New York Times lauded the firm for offering one year, one-third salary furloughs to their associates. What a gift! Unfortunately, like youth, it is wasted on the young. Associates will enjoy the sabbatical, but it is the older partners who need it. For them, time off, forced or not, would be a marvelous, perhaps once in a lifetime, opportunity. The truly wise might consider counseling to compound in personal growth the value of the gift.

Life is short and for the 50ish law firm partner the time for needed change draws near. At 1,800+ billable hours there has scarcely been time to catch one's breath let alone consider the suitability of the structure of one's life and the wisdom of its direction. In ten years the average partner will begin the transition from middle to old age, with all the changes then required whether wanted or not. Ten years after that, time will truly be running out, if it has not already done so. One will have achieved the biblical three score and ten and though medicine may keep us alive considerably longer, all but a few of the good years will have been spent.

The life of the busy private practice lawyer goes by so quickly that the speed itself can create the illusion of progress. Matters are opened and closed, trials won and lost, long hours are worked, bonuses are sought, awarded and appealed, weeks and months slide by, years disappear. In reality, the only progress here is financial and some increase, diminishing with experience, in expertise. The toll upon the self may be only dimly perceived, perhaps utterly ignored.

Using Transitional Periods to Evaluate Life Structure

While each period in life has distinct challenges derived from its location in the life cycle, all the transitional periods share in common the need to evaluate life structure and revise it. Our research has shown that a life structure can only be satisfactory for about seven years, nine at the most. After that, stagnation sets in. Occurring roughly every ten years and lasting for several, we spend a great deal of our lives in transitions. What we make of the opportunities they provide usually depends upon the help we receive.

The Mid-Life Transition

The best known of the transitional periods is the mid-life transition. It occurs in the years around 40, halfway through the life cycle. My mentor, Daniel Levinson, and his colleagues, discovered it in the early 1970s at Yale University in research on adult development. The findings from this research have been widely disseminated in popular publications.

Although the transitional periods from one era to the next—around 20, 40, 60 and 80—tend to be the most challenging, there are other important transitions in the life cycle as well, including one around fifty. We called this *the age fifty transition* and it, too, is consequential. It is the last period in the life cycle when nature helps us change before old age descends.

The Age 50 Transition

At 50, a person is halfway through the era of middle age. This time deserves special attention because it is important in the demography of authority, typical, as mentioned, of most law firm managing partners (52), CFOs (49), CEOs (54) in various enterprises, and American presidents (55). At fifty, there remains sufficient time and ordinarily enough vigor for significant change. However, one's wishes may not be a reliable guide. After years of self-denial, neglected wishes accumulate force like waves that travel unobstructed over vast expanses of the ocean, and they can overwhelm reason. Great fiction dramatizes the negative consequences, and we see these in real life, too.

Take, for example, von Aschenbach, in Thomas Mann's novel, *Death in Venice*. Aschenbach is an acclaimed writer in his early fifties. He lives in Munich and ordinarily goes to the mountains for his vacation, but this year he feels disinclined to stay with tradition. Of a sudden he is overcome with the wish for a new existence, a craving for freedom, a break from the rigid, cold and exhausting work of the past thirty years. The sunny, exotic South beckons and he goes to Venice. There he encounters Tadzio, an untouchable incarnation of his vanished youth, and falls in love assailed by the reality of his own decay.

He might have been happier in the mountains.

Don Quixote was bordering 49 when he set off in pursuit of an over-ripe dream of becoming a knight-errant. It was a fine dream but one whose hero had grown too old for it, and so he tilted at windmills and generally made himself ridiculous.

Arguably, it would have been better if he had stayed at home.

Based upon historical documents, the actual Macbeth of Shakespeare's play appears to have been in his late forties when he took the fulfillment of his dynastic dreams into his own bloody hands, and in his fifties when he destroyed his ill-gotten reign with pre-emptive paranoid savagery.

Wouldn't he have been wiser to have contented himself with the promotion to Thane of Cawdor and left it at that?

At around 50, George W. Bush decided to pursue the presidency.

Where we find examples of individuals who achieve triumphant mid-life change, such persons have usually had the benefit of developmental counsel, formal or informal. They appear less frequently in great fiction than in life because the dramatic possibilities of happiness are limited.

Freud, for example, used a mid-life crisis to leave neurology—at the time a field, as he put it, in which one could only make diagnoses and these could only be confirmed by autopsy—for psychoanalysis. His close friend and colleague, Wilhelm Fliess, helped him face the difficulties of the change. Freud then stayed creatively engaged in building his new theoretical and clinical enterprise for the remainder of a long life.

Sherwood Anderson, the American writer, had a dramatic mid-life crisis, featuring a dissociative fugue that carried him from business and a bad marriage to the life of a writer successfully pursuing a long neglected dream.

Gandhi used his late forties to make the transition from British barrister to transformative Indian political and religious leader—the Mahatma— conducting his nonviolent civil disobedience campaign in his early 50s.

And there are others.

Help in Revising Life Structure

It has been said that one should never waste a crisis. President Obama, at 48, seemed to embody this dictum, as he struck forth weekly to meet some unmet national challenge, from the regulation and rescue of financial markets, to immigration, health care, education, international relations, nuclear disarmament, piracy, simplifying the tax code, transportation and more. In doing so, Obama got lots of help, or at least advice.

When laid off, partners may seek outplacement counseling but usually limit its scope simply to finding another job. In so doing, they lose the opportunity for an inquiry into the state of their dreams and the health of their inner selves: "What did I want when I set out upon this path 25 years ago; do I still want the same thing? What matters most to me now? Am I living my life properly, or am I wasting it? What makes me happiest? What is best in me and what room have I made for its expression in the life I am living? How many good years remain, and how should I spend them?"

A good referral is needed to find a counselor who is competent to help with these questions. Most outplacement counselors are simply headhunters, untrained in psychology and only superficially in touch with their own psyches. Those who cannot face their own midlife questions, or who are too young to know about them, may avoid raising them with you. Occasionally a close friend or family member can perform this role, but too often their stake in the outcome of the transition acts as a limiting bias. A friend may need you to validate his choices, a family member to stay in harness.

Even if the result of the inventory of self and life is a decision to resume commitments, the process of inquiry with a skilled, resonant counselor will have shifted the meanings or clarified them. Holding course with a renewed sense of purpose can put the wind back in one's sails.

The New York Times writer reporting the Skadden Arps initiative concluded, "Sometimes it takes getting thrown out of the office to notice that there is a life outside." Getting thrown out of the office can help an attorney notice that there is a life inside, too.

"Never waste a crisis." Brave words, but most of us need help to live them.

2. Career Review: The Cases of Alan and Richard

Long-term economic studies show that 'downsizing' does not save money in the long run. Nonetheless, firm leaders are under great pressure to lay off employees at the first sign of revenue trouble. This means even longtime partners may be asked to leave the firm.

The stereotype of the CEO depicts a rational bottom-liner unencumbered by fellow feeling. In reality, few executives lay off employees comfortably, although we note as exceptions presidential aspirants Mitt Romney who famously declared that he liked to fire people and Donald Trump who makes a television show of terminating people, perhaps in anticipation of being president.

Most dread the prospect. In fact, some remain distressed many years later. Occasionally, a CEO`s good feeling about his job never fully returns, and the event becomes a turning point in his own life as well as in the lives of the people he has let go. In a few cases, the executive suffers from a post-traumatic stress disorder, including the intrusive return of memories of termination interviews with a devastated employee.

As noted, for some laid off employees, a psychological choice between depression and anger is posed, and studies show that domestic violence is related to job stress, especially demotion or termination. In a predisposed individual, the reaction to job loss can be floridly psychopathological.

Healthier people react to being laid off with depression rather than paranoid anger. The depressed are healthier in the sense that they internalize the problem and try to work it out, rather than yielding to the temptation to blame others and get even, if only in fantasy. Nonetheless the depressive approach of exaggerating one's own failure involves needless suffering and can lead to its own dangerous extremes, such as excessive drinking, reckless driving, and other self-destructive acts.

The Case of Alan

The challenge both for the newly jobless individual and for former employers offering help is to understand the employment termination not as an ending, but as a beginning, one which initiates a transitional period in the person's life. This transitional period should be used to chart new and better directions.

Consider the following case. It is an example of a depressive reaction.

Alan was a 50-year-old partner of a large, full-service firm. His practice area was insurance defense, an area that his firm had been de-emphasizing for several years because of billing rate pressures from clients. When the economy slowed and showed alarming signs of a serious downturn, his firm asked him and some others in his practice group to leave. In a sense, this had been as inevitable as the business cycle, yet Alan had wanted to believe that his partners wouldn't do this to him. The news came to him as a painful surprise. As part of Alan's termination from the firm, the managing partner offered him outplacement counseling, which he accepted.

When I met with Alan, he was depressed, angry and lost. He felt hurt by his colleagues but mainly critical of himself. He said that he saw himself as having failed at what had been the most important thing to him. He compared himself to others in the firm and came out the loser, left witless, without what mattered most. He spoke of waking up in the night near panic, when he realized that he would soon have no office to go to, no clients to serve. He asked himself how, if by 50 he had failed to create a successful work life, would he ever do so? He described days in which he felt like a miserable failure, asking himself over and over, "How did I get into such a mess?"

During several interviews, we traced Alan's career backward in time. He said that it had been some years since he had really enjoyed his work. Somehow, he had ended up doing more work for the clients he enjoyed least and less work with the ones he liked best. Although he had kept his billable hours up, the erosion in his profitability year by year had been

166

eroding his own sense of value. His work, he now realized, had become so commoditized that he had been feeling less like a professional than a clerk.

What he had lost in the termination, it now became clear, was not important work but the feeling of importance that came from being a well-paid partner in a good firm. The rewards for his work had become increasingly extrinsic and its connection to his self more and more distant. He could now see that his termination from his firm constituted not a sudden departure but a landmark on a trail that had been going downhill for several years.

The Path Not Taken

Often in adult lives there is a path not taken that retains its significance. I asked Alan what he would have done, if he had not gone to law school. At first, Alan had trouble thinking about the question and answered it in the way many lawyers do: "When I graduated from college, I didn't know what I wanted to do, so I went to law school." Encouraged to think about the matter more deeply, Alan recalled that in his late teens and early 20s he had had a nascent dream of going to sea, which his father had done as a career naval officer. His parents discouraged this. They wanted more lucrative employment for their oldest son. During his 30-year career, Alan had relegated his dream to the status of a sailing hobby that he and his wife enjoyed. Indeed, they had hoped someday to retire to a life of cruising in Mexico, where the weather is warm and the living cheap.

Upon being terminated from his firm, Alan's inclination was to go straight to a recruiter. Now, he had second thoughts. He realized he did not want to get a job doing exactly what he had been doing, and that he needed more time to find a better way. He was not ready to make a choice that might lock him in for the remainder of his working life.

Instead, Alan and his wife decided to take a sabbatical and allow themselves time to consider next steps in a more leisurely manner. Why not, Alan asked: the children were grown, educated, and living independently? The couple's mortgage was small, and the home could be rented out-- to law firm associates as it would turn out-- at a substantial price. The difference between mortgage and rent would cover outfitting their sloop to make it more seaworthy and comfortable and cover the living costs of as much as a year cruising the coasts of Baja California and mainland Mexico.

The Case of Richard

Not every outplacement counseling ends with idyllic new choices. Most results are more prosaic, at least as viewed from the outside. Consider the case of Richard. His is an example of a more paranoid reaction.

A civil litigator, Richard had been with the same firm since law school. He was now 55 and over the years had served the firm in various ways: as a mentor to young lawyers, two stints as managing partner, and as a reliable rainmaker.

Richard's firm operated by consensus. This meant that when a strong leader had been in power, like Richard, some growth occurred. The managing partner who followed Richard had little inclination to lead and the partnership napped its way into over reliance on a few large clients. Richard observed his successor's failure and predicted the firm's increasing vulnerability. He made indications to important partners that he was ready to serve again, if asked, but his overtures were not returned.

Unexpectedly, one of the firm's major clients announced it was leaving the state. This woke up firm owners and led to the realization that they needed to run it like a business, but Richard was not named managing partner. Instead, the firm recruited a lateral partner with an MBA.

Richard quickly found himself at odds with the new managing partner over management style and philosophy. Before long, the partnership became divided and immobilized with conflict. Unable to resolve their differences and create a reasonable working relationship, the managing partner, with executive committee approval, asked Richard to leave. As part of the severance offer, Richard was given outplacement counseling.

When I saw him, Richard was nearly speechless with outrage. "After all I've done for the firm, this little pip-squeak comes along and orders me out. And the partners go along with it!" He bitterly claimed that partners who were supposedly friends were paying him back for "tough decisions" he had made for the good of the firm. Richard spoke bitterly of a rival rainmaker in another practice group who he imagined was behind the move. It seemed to Richard that his man had hated him ever since he'd blocked his "girlfriend's" promotion to partnership.

Richard vowed to get back at the firm by going to the legal press, airing dirty laundry about a botched case, and driving their biggest clients away. He swore that he would not allow his "old friends and sleazy leaders" to betray and attack him and get away with it.

After Richard cooled down, we began a career review. What we found was that Richard had not been happy or comfortable in the firm since he had stepped down the last time as managing partner five years earlier. Though he had remained influential, he did not really like being out of power, and he did not like, nor value, the skills needed to be effective behind the scenes. He liked having power legitimately and being able to exercise it openly. The more subtle style of subsequent managing partners in the firm, especially the new business school types, had made him uneasy and suspicious. He found them viscous and untrustworthy.

Leaderly Inclinations

Richard was a natural leader. Throughout his life, he had enjoyed running things. He had been student body president in college and a leader in law school. He had been active in the state bar association and had held elective office in the community in which he and his wife lived.

He began to understand that his conflict with the new managing partner was not primarily philosophical or personal. A new generation of leadership, men and women in their 40s, was taking over the firm and people in their mid- to late 50s and early 60s were finding themselves set aside.

Richard had thought he had stepped aside gracefully when he had left the managing partner position. Now he began to recall occasion after occasion when he had opposed and obstructed - *always for the best reasons, only on the merits!* - new leadership over the past five years and that this had finally come to a head. It was simply in the cards that Richard had either to temper his desire for power and truly step aside or leave.

Richard had long imagined opening his own firm and running it the way he wanted. He had been kept from doing so by his attachment to his old firm and by the gratification of his own importance within it. He admitted that he had also been afraid that he might fail. Clearer about what he wanted and no longer wasting energy in angry fantasies of revenge, Richard now decided to open a real estate litigation boutique and successfully recruit some young lawyers from another firm to join him. They found suitable space, signed a lease agreement and set up shop.

In the end, Richard felt relieved that he had restrained himself from acts of revenge against his old firm. The firm meant a great deal to him and to hurt it would have been to hurt himself. Public controversy might also have soiled the new firm he was starting. Instead, he was content with the civilized satisfaction of the future possibility of defeating his old partners in court.

Reappraisal Counseling

Because the best result of outplacement counseling is not always knowable at the beginning, precipitous decisions need to be avoided. Psychologically wiser choices ordinarily require several in-depth interviews. A person may need to go in-house, on his or her own, choose to practice a similar kind of law in a similar firm, make a radical departure in kind and setting of practice, take up another line of work and so on. What matters most is that the lawyer engages in a genuine reappraisal of his or her work life and of his or her own real self, considers alternatives, and makes an examined choice.

The future is always uncertain, but taking ones inner self seriously and acting with courage restores and sustains pride. Asked to identify the capacities that would characterize a healthy person, Freud answered "Lieben und Arbeiten," the ability to love and to work. Freud meant to love and to work in a truly engaged manner, not in a timid, obligatory way. Done with psychological skill and sophistication, outplacement counseling should lead to a decision that better connects self and work, mobilizes the attorney's creative energy, and restores zest to living.

3. Retirement: A Developmental Task

Retirement is not an event but a process occurring within the context of an unfolding life. To think clearly about retirement and decide what to do, we must consider the nature of old age as an era in the life cycle and retirement as part of the transition to it.

We tend to imagine the stages beyond the one in which we are currently living as featureless plateaus or cliffs. In the view of the 20 year old, 40 and everything beyond is simply "old." For the 40 year old, 60 is *truly* old and can contain little beyond retirement, debility, and death. Yet for those who endure to see it, the sixties and seventies constitute a new era, qualitatively different from a later stage, which begins around 80. We might call this last the "Final Era."

Our age parochialism leaves us unprepared upon reaching 60 to find again the variegated terrain that stretches out ahead, full of unexpected opportunities, challenges, and dilemmas. Even the most thoughtful and observant among us can be caught unaware. At 74 Freud wrote a friend, "The idea of a peaceful old age is turning out to be as much of a myth as that of a happy childhood."

Some are cheered, others wearied, to find at 60 that one is not really old. Unless an illness or injury with enduring consequences has intervened, one has sufficient strength not merely for quiet pastimes like bridge, lawn bowling and golf, but for active sports like bicycling, squash, weight lifting and swimming. One retains plenty of libido for sex and embarrassingly high levels of romantic yearning and illusion, pride and resentment, passions still strongly resembling their earlier editions.

When a loss of energy seems to occur, it may result from an absence of inspiration and the presence of stultifying structure at home and at work and in one's relationship to one's self. Too often we passively choose to be dominated by stereotype and ritual in relating to friends and family; to hold beliefs about the self that do little more than fend off anxiety and corral doubt; and, to be addicted to mind numbing, soporific drugs such as alcohol and television.

When we read serious fiction and biography, we imagine and remember; when we sleep, we dream. In both cases psychological work gets done.

Television lowers mental activity to a level just above coma. It empties then fills a space that ought to be occupied by the mind.

An Invariant Life Cycle

How could a bountiful seniority be possible? Would it be because, as we now hear, "60 is the new 40," and "80 the new 60?" It appeals to our narcissism to think that our cohort is new and special, elevated above the generations that have preceded it. Similarly, the companion illusion that people are living longer now than ever before pleases us. Closer inspection reveals that actually 60 is more or less the same as it has always been and the life span has not elongated by more than a few years.

We are not healthier now than when we were hopping around a campfire living active lives. Indeed, our sedentary existence creates the modern prevalence of obesity, diabetes, and heart disease, and these together with environmental cancer, and the mechanized lethalities of travel and warfare, have nullified many of the advantages that scientific medicine and the absence of animal predators have given us.

Increased Average Life Expectancy, not Longer Life Span

Paleodemographic data on this point seem clear: People are not living longer, but in the developed countries more people are living a long time. Thus, while the life span has not lengthened, *average* life expectancy has increased as a result of declines in infant and maternal mortality. If one survives the first year of life, and if a woman survives her childbearing years, life expectancy is not much different than it has been for tens, possibly hundreds, of thousands of years.

Each of the eras up to 60—those of pre-adulthood, early adulthood and middle age—has begun with a transitional period. So does the era of old age. The years ~60-65 form a transitional time bridging middle and old age. In these years, a person is becoming one of the "young old." Each of the previous eras has also contained a mid-era transitional period. So does this one. In the years around 70, the person will become "mid-old." At around 80, in the transition from the era of old age to the final era, one becomes "old old."

The Young Old

The primary task of this period is to leave the life lived in middle age and make choices for a fresh life structure that will meet the challenges of the new era in a positive way. Throughout youth and middle age, a central component of the life structure for attorneys has been work. Moving from a life centered upon full time work to one with partial involvement in it or none at all is what is meant by retirement.

The other central component of the life structure has typically been taking care of children. Here, too, the loss of an important role takes place as one's children become independent adults. Though we like to make jokes about the joys of getting them off the payroll, in fact their independence threatens to make us feel useless and unloved.

4. Doing Psychological Work on Retirement

A central task of the previous transitions has been to refashion dreams into a life structure suitable for the coming era. By dreams, I refer not to the nocturnal
variety but to the life goals in which we invest our most deeply cherished hopes.

Dreams at Twenty

For the person turning 20, dreams were formed in childhood and modified during adolescence. In the latter period, dreams take on a tint of adulthood, but in fact remain heavily colored by the unrealistic wishes and fears of the earliest years. The Oedipus complex and its mix of heroic striving and generational conflict is the most famous of these underlying puerile schemas.

One enters each transitional period as a novice. The 20 year old knows more about early adulthood than the neonate knows about infancy, but much of what the young man or woman 'knows' is thin, poorly understood and borrowed not lived. When I reread some of the great literature I first encountered at 20, I realize that if I had understood it better, I might not have been able to read it. In the same way, it has been said that if children knew what their parent's lives were really like, they would not have the courage to grow up.

The 20 year old looks for a part of the adult world in which he or she can make a good enough beginning. "Good enough" means viable in the world and suitable to the self. This is a momentous challenge and one at which many fail and some cannot even attempt. Once found, the young person becomes a member of the *Entering Generation*.

Dreams at Forty

At 40, a person has advanced another full step up the generational ladder. He or she is entering middle age and can see the results of the heroic quests, or timid conformities, of youth. He is entering the *Leadership Generation* of the sector of society in which he works. At this point, one knows one's way around the adult world and has developed an adult self with which one is familiar.

No longer able to stake a claim simply on strength and beauty, and less likely now to conquer the world or even one's profession, what sort of an inspiring vision suitable for middle age can an attorney find among the embers left in the crucible of youth? Without a reformed dream, the obligations taken on when young will be a very heavy burden indeed, with duty having to serve where fresh inspiration is needed.

Dreams at Sixty

At around 60, the attorney's occupational tide is ebbing. He or she is now a member of the *Retiring Generation*. While still capable of 200 billable hour months and of legal expertise of the highest order, the question "What's the point?" intrudes itself with increasing insistence. If "the point" is that one does not know what else to do, we have the makings of a rough passage in the transition from middle to old age.

The 60 year old, notwithstanding his or her experience and wisdom, enters old age as a beginner, too. The senior lawyer understands that he is to 'wind down" his professional work, to "transition his practice," to "move toward" retirement, and to look forward to "enjoying the fruits of his labor." But these are only clichés that gloss over the inevitable incompetence as to how and when to do these things. There is also the frightening cultural and psychological equation of retirement with death, an equation that finds some reality in the actuarial tables.

In fact, for most 60 year olds in the developed countries and often enough elsewhere, dying is a task that will not be encountered until the final era that begins around 80, some 20 years and more off.

The problem at 60 is not death but the *number of good years* remaining and what one wants to do with them.

It's hard to give up doing something that one is very good at to be a mediocre golfer, a clumsy volunteer, or a hovering nuisance to one's spouse and grown children. The blow to self-esteem and narcissism is huge. And since one's very success at a demanding profession has testified to the strength of the daemon that drives us, how will we appease it if we are no longer "productive?"

What Does My Work Amount To?

Clearly psychological work is needed and there is no better place to start than with the question of the value of one's work.

As noted, successful transitions require this sort of reappraisal. "How did I get here; what and who have I become; what did I want, what do I really care about now; what have I done to and for others—parents, siblings, spouses, children, friends, clients, my profession, society? Have I realized what is best in me? Do I leave behind anything of value beyond the material?"

Making lists or adding up one's retirement accounts cannot answer questions of this sort. Money matters but there is no magic number that will tell us when we should retire, let alone what we should do afterwards. Television, airport novels and self-help books are not likely to help much either. There is no longer time for page-turners; what is needed are attention-arresters.

Courage will have to be summoned to attend more fully to the inner voices—to think, remember, imagine, dream, talk honestly with friends, socialize with interesting people who are doing interesting things, read great fiction and good biography where one can see how others have worked on problems whose underlying nature is universal but whose variations expand our sense of what is possible. Getting coaching for retirement may be needed as well.

Accepting Oneself and One's Life

The trick is to engage in the necessary psychological work without becoming overly self-critical. Each person has rather good reasons for being who he is. One could certainly have done better, but for most of us hard working and responsible people, perhaps not much better. Indeed, given the limitations of our backgrounds and the flaws within our personalities, it may be rather remarkable that we have done as well as we have.

Looking back on his life from the age of 87, Leonard Woolf, Virginia's husband—accomplished writer, social critic and political activist—said that he could see no major political issue or social problem upon which he had had any significant effect. He notes this not with harsh self-disapproval, but with the temperate objectivity of an 87 year old.

In fact, few, very few of us live lives that matter to any but a small circle of those close to us. So what? When history takes a sanguine turn, positive change occurs in society, or when our professions improve this is usually the result of unseen, even uncontrollable forces, and of accident.

Even the good works of the great may end up serving destructive purposes.

At the end of his life Karl Marx, disgusted by the revolutionary politics practiced in his name, cried out, "I am not a Marxist!" Freud lamented that his followers were "docile analysts," who were turning his suggestions for a humane and flexible treatment into rigid dogma. Indeed, he would not now be considered a Freudian. Einstein was horrified by the practical consequences of his theoretical work. Oppenheimer said after the explosion of the atomic bomb that physicists "had known sin." He quoted the *Bhagavad-Gita*, "Now I am become Death, the destroyer of worlds."

To consider less lofty levels of achievement, Hillary Clinton tells us that Bill is the most popular person in the world. Coke and Big Macs are even better liked. What does this sort of success signify beyond tooth decay, heart disease, diabetes, and self-aggrandizement? Should we consider our achievements inadequate next to these?

At 69, having failed to retire, Hillary offered herself as the second oldest president in our history. Her victorious opponent, having become the oldest president in our history, besieged us with senile narcissism and even when we retired him, refused to retire. President Joe Biden teeters at the end of the age distribution having entered the Final Era.

Bibliography

Bayes, Marjorie and Newton, Peter M., Women in authority: A sociopsychological approach. *Journal of Applied Behavioral Science,* 1978, *14,* 7-20. Reprinted in Coleman and Geller (Eds.), *Group Relations Reader,* Washington, D.C.: A. K. Rice Institute, 1986. Reprinted by *Conference Board.*

Bion, Wilfred, *Experiences in Groups,* Tavistock Publications, 1959.

Collins, James & Porras, Jerry, Built to Last: Successful Habits of Visionary Companies, Harper Business, 1994.

Durkheim, Emile, *Rules of the Sociological Method,* The Free Press, 1982. *The Division of Labor in Society,* The Free Press, 1960. *Suicide,* The Free Press, 1951.

Eagle, Jeffrey and Newton, Peter M., Scapegoating in small groups: An organizational approach. *Human Relations,* 1981, *34,* 283-301.

Goffman, Erving, *Asylums,* Doubleday Anchor, 1961. *Relations in Public,* Basic Books, 1971.

Goldratt, E. *The Goal,* North River Press, 1992.

Hirschhorn, Larry, *The Psychodynamics of Organizations,* Temple University Press, 1993.

Howenstine, R., Silberstein, L., Newton, D., & Newton, P., Revitalizing the life structure: An adult developmental approach to psychodynamic psychotherapy. *Psychiatry, Interpersonal and Biological Processes,* 1992, *55,* 94-106.

Jaques, E., *Requisite Organization,* Cason Hall, 1989. *Work, Creativity, and Social Justice,* Heinemann, 1970. *Executive Leadership* (with Clement & Lessem), Wiley, 1994.

Hodgson, Richard C., Levinson, Daniel J., & Zaleznik, Abraham, *The Executive Role Constellation,* Harvard University Press, 1965.

Kafka, Franz, *The Trial,* Schocken, 1999.

Levinson, Daniel J. *The Seasons of a Man's Life,* Knopf, 1977. *The Seasons of a Woman's Life,* Knopf, 1996. Role, personality and social structure within the organizational setting, *Journal of Abnormal and Social Psychology,* 1959, *58,* 170-180.

Lohser, Beate and Newton, Peter M., *Unorthodox Freud: The View from the Couch,* New York: The Guilford Press, 1996.

Miller, E. J., & Rice, A. K., *Systems of Organization,* Tavistock Publications, 964.

Maister, David H. *Managing the Professional Service Firm,* New York: Free Press, 1993.

Mann, Thomas. *The Magic Mountain,* Vintage, 1996.

Newton, Peter M., Abstinence as a role requirement in psychotherapy. *Psychiatry: Journal for the Study of Interpersonal Processes,* 1971, *34,* 391-400. Reprinted in Langs, R. (Ed.), *The Therapeutic Interaction,* Vol. 1. New York: Jason Aronson, Inc., 1976. Reprinted in *Cathexis.* 1981, *4,* 109-121.

Newton, Peter M. and Levinson, Daniel J., The work group within the organization: A sociopsychological approach. *Psychiatry: Journal for the Study of Interpersonal Processes,* 1973, *35,* 115-142. Reprinted in Dumas, R., *Staff Training Manual,* National Institute of Mental Health Documents, 1976.

Newton, Peter M., Social structure and process in psychotherapy: A socio-psychological analysis of transference, resistance and change. *International Journal of Psychiatry,* 1973, *11,* 480-512.

Newton, Peter M., Author's reply. *International Journal of Psychiatry,* 1973, *11,* 523-52.

Newton, Peter M., *Obedience to Authority* by Stanley Milgram. A review, *American Scientist,* 1974, *62,* 476-477.

Newton, Peter M., Seasons of a Man's Life, a review. American Scientist, 1978, 66, 630.

Newton, Peter M. and Levinson, Daniel J., Crises in adult development. Chapter 36 in Lazare, Aaron (Ed.), *Outpatient Psychiatry,* Baltimore: Williams and Wilkins, 1979.

Newton, Peter M., The accursed correspondence: The Freud-Jung letters. *University Publishing,* Spring, 1979.

Newton, Peter M., Who among us still hopes to learn more about the nature of man? *University Publishing,* Winter, 1981.

Newton, Peter M., Periods in the adult development of the faculty member. *Human Relations,* 1983, *36,* 441-458.

Newton, Peter M., Samuel Johnson's breakdown and recovery in middle-age: A life span developmental approach to mental illness and its cure. *International Review of Psycho-Analysis,* 1984, *11,* 93-118.

Newton, Peter M., Science and humanism in the biographical study of lives. *Contemporary Psychiatry,* 1988, *7,* 77-81.

Newton, Peter M., Free association and the division of labor in psychoanalytic treatment. *Psychoanalytic Psychology,* 1989, *6,* 31-46.

Newton, Peter M., A social system approach to the psychoanalytic treatment of personality disorders. *Psychiatry, Interpersonal and Biological Processes,* 1992, *55,* 66 78.

Newton, Peter M., Freud's mid-life crisis. *Psychoanalytic Psychology,* 1992, *9,* 447 475.

Newton, Peter M., Daniel Levinson and his theory of adult development: A reminiscence and some clarifications. *Journal of Adult Development,* 1994, *1,* 135 147.

Newton, Peter M., Freud's development in early adulthood and our own. *Journal of the Northern California Society for Psychoanalytic Psychology,* Fall, 1994, 36-40.

Newton, Peter M., *Freud: From Youthful Dream to Mid-Life Crisis,* New York: The Guilford Press, 1995.

Newton, Peter M. and Newton, Dorian S., Erik Erikson. Chapter 2, In Kaplan, Harold & Sadock, Benjamin (Eds.,) *The Comprehensive Textbook of Psychiatry,* 6th Edition. Baltimore: Williams & Wilkins, 1995, pp. 478-486.

Newton, Peter M., Some suggestions for the conduct of biographical research. *Journal of Adult Development,* 1995, *2,* 147-158.

Newton, Peter M. and Gersick, Kellin. Daniel J. Levinson (1920-94). *American Psychologist,* 1996, *51,* 262.

Newton, Peter M. Reply to Holt. *Psychoanalytic Books,* 1996, *7,* 295-298.

Newton, Peter M. A last word. *Psychoanalytic Books,* 1996, *7,* 447-451.

Newton, Peter M. Review of *Sándor Ferenczi. Psychoanalytic Books,* 1998, *9,* 429 435.

Newton, Peter M. and Lohser, Beate. Reply to Makari. *International Journal of Psycho-Analysis,* 1998, *79,* 103-104.

Newton, Peter M. Review of Intimate Attachments. Psychoanalytic Books, 1999, 10,76-82.

Newton, Peter M. Trivializing the mentor relationship. *Legal Week, May* 13, 1999.

Newton, Dorian S. and Newton, Peter M., Erik Erikson. In Kaplan, Harold & Sadock, Benjamin (Eds.,) *The Comprehensive Textbook of Psychiatry,* 7th Edition. Baltimore: Williams & Wilkins, 2000.

Newton, Peter M. Problem personalities or problematic organizations? *Law Firm Partnership and Benefits Report,* Summer, 2000.

Newton, Peter M. Mentoring the young refreshes senior executives. *Executive Talent,* 2000, *1,* 12-13.

Newton, Peter M. Ending the Exodus. *American Lawyer,* January 2001.

Newton, Peter M. The Chain of Command: Management Principles for Managing Partners, *Managing Partner,* September 2001.

Newton, Peter M. *Management Thoughtletters,* Volume I, 2005.

Newton, Peter M. *Management Thoughtletters,* Volume II, 2006.

Newton, Peter M. *Management Thoughtletters*, Volume III, 2007.

Newton, Peter M. *Management Thoughtletters,* Volume IV, 2008.

Newton, Peter M. *Management Thoughtletters,* Volume V, 2009.

Roberts, Priscilla and Newton, Peter M., Levinsonian studies of women's adult development. *Psychology and Aging,* 1987, *2,* 154-163. Reprinted in Hudson, Merle (Ed.), *Psychology of Adulthood and Aging,* Burnaby, B.C., Canada: Open Learning Agency, 1994.

Sloane, A. *My Years with General Motors,* Doubleday, 1990.

Smelser & Smelser, *Personality and Social Systems,* Wiley, 1963.

Snow, David L. and Newton, Peter M., Task, social structure and social process in the community mental health center movement. *American Psychologist,* 1976, *32,*
582-594.

Weiss, A. Getting Started In Consulting, Wiley, 2003. Value-Based Fees, Pfeiffer,
2002.

Index

G

Gandhi, Mahatma, 163

G.B. Shaw, 35

Gardner, Chauncy see Chauncy
Gardner

Gauguin, 89

gender, xix, xxv, 6, 49, 56, 92, 110,
123

generation, xxx, 2, 13, 36, 47, 48,
49, 59, 69, 80, 100, 119, 132,
133, 141,155, 156, 157, 158, 170,
173, 175, 176

George W. Bush, 65, 148, 162

good values rationalization, xx, 103,
111

Goodwin, Doris see Doris Goodwin

Great Recession of 2008, 159

Greenspan, Alan see Alan
Greenspan

group boundaries, 111

H

Hamilton, Booz Allen see Booz
Allen Hamilton

Hamlet, 49

Harding, 69

Harris, Kamala see Kamala Harris

Harvard Business Review, 63

Henry Adams, 86

Hewlett-Packard, 142, 143

H. G. Wells, 52

Hillary Clinton, 69, 70, 178

Hitler, 72, 94

I

identification, 40, 67, 92, 102

internalization, 86, 88

J

Jack Welch, 94, 108

Jefferson, 69

Johnson, 69, 183

judgmentalism, 3, 6

K

Kamala Harris, 69

Karl Marx, 178

Kennedy, John F. *see President
Kennedy*

Kennedy, Robert *see Robert
Kennedy*

King Frederick the Great, 55

L

lateral, 27, 28, 29, 62, 109, 156, 168

life cycle, 2, 13, 49, 155, 156, 157,
158, 160, 161, 171

Lincoln, Abraham *see Abraham
Lincoln*

M

Macbeth, 162

managing partner, xvii, xix, xxi,
xxv, xxvi, xxx, 5, 6, 7, 8, 9, 10,
14, 15, 16, 17, 18, 20, 21, 26, 27,
28, 29, 33, 59, 61, 65, 66, 73, 77,
78, 88, 89, 100, 104, 116, 117,
127, 129, 130, 133, 134, 136,
137, 139, 140, 141, 142, 158,
161, 166, 168, 169, 170

www.ingramcontent.com/pod-product-compliance
Lightning Source LLC
Chambersburg PA
CBHW070346300526
45791CB00023B/179

9 781517 062057